Museums Discovered: The Isabella Stewart Gardner Museum

Edited by Eve Sinaiko

Editorial staff: Sandra Moy,
Alison de Lima Greene, and
Anthony Strianse

Color photography by Greg Heins
Photographs on pages 21-27, 41, 45, 57,
65, 73, 99, 107-111, 118, 119, 125, 179,
and 201 by Herbert Vose.

ISBN: 0-934516-44-8
Library of Congress Card Catalog Number: 81-50895

Created for Woodbine Books, Inc. by
Shorewood Fine Art Books
475 Tenth Avenue
New York, N.Y. 10018

Plates 97, *Madame Gaujelin* and 99, *Leaving the Paddock*,
by Edgar Degas; 117, *The Terrace, St.-Tropez*,
by Henri Matisse; and 118, *Costume for Ida Rubinstein*
and 119 *Costume for Anna Pavlova*, by Léon Bakst, reproduced
courtesy of S.P.A.D.E.M., Paris, and V.A.G.A., New York.

Museums Discovered: The Isabella Stewart Gardner Museum

by Rollin van N. Hadley

Woodbine Books
Ft. Lauderdale, Florida

Created by Shorewood Fine Art Books
New York

Introduction

Over the main entrance to the Isabella Stewart Gardner Museum, a coat of arms is carved in relief on a stone plaque: a phoenix rising from the ashes with the motto *C'est Mon Plaisir*. The phoenix is the symbol of the renewal of life, and the motto, of course, Mrs. Gardner's personal creed. Her pleasure and capricious taste are still evident today. Although she has been the subject of many biographies, the museum is her true reflection. By the terms of her will no work of art may be added to these galleries, and the general arrangement must remain as she left it. It clearly states that the museum is to be for the education and enjoyment of the public forever. Her success with this remarkable creation, frozen in time, is as convincing today as on that winter's night when it was first seen by Boston society.

Visitors today, as on that first night, do not enter by the main door opposite the courtyard, but by a small, rather plain door off to one side. The element of surprise, so dear to Mrs. Gardner, begins from that moment and continues almost every step of the way. The Spanish Cloister, just inside the public entrance, is a mixture of medieval sculpture, Italian ironwork, and Mexican tiles leading to Sargent's dramatic painting of the flamenco dance, *El Jaleo,* positioned under a Moorish arch. From this quiet setting, with its eclectic, unpredictable arrangement, the visitor is suddenly aware of the brilliant flower-filled courtyard beyond.

This court is the focus of the building. Rising four stories to a glass roof, the space provides light and enjoyment from every angle. The court is filled with classical sculpture, the one exception being a Venetian fountain at the far end. In all four facades are windows, balconies, and reliefs taken from the exteriors of Venetian *palazzi;* through the windows visitors may catch a glimpse of a gallery beyond, often with a calculated view of a particular picture or group of objects, positioned so as to be seen across the court. Here, the faint sound of falling water, the fragrance of flowers, and the changing light from the sky combine to entrance those who stop in the cloisters that enclose this garden.

The cloisters, with marble sculpture and ironwork—railings, gates, and *torchères*—under vaulted ceilings, have marble columns and capitals supporting the arches. The arrangement here and throughout the museum is not chronological or by country, but designed purely to enhance the objects. Some consistency may be seen in the groupings of pictures; for example, almost all nineteenth- and twentieth-century paintings are in the small rooms across the front of the ground floor. Some are of great quality, the work of Manet and Degas, while others are the work of painters who were friends of Mrs. Gardner, artists whom she wished to encourage or who made her a present of a chosen picture.

All the galleries of the second and third floors are

Fenway Court

in the manner of a great Italian villa, with the accumulation of generations dispersed in a seemingly haphazard fashion. All are different in feeling, but in fact are carefully arranged to produce this effect. Four large galleries on the north front of the museum, two on each floor above the first, contain the majority of the Italian paintings for which the collection is best known. Early Italian gold-ground panels are hung on white plaster or rough panelling, while High Renaissance and Baroque paintings are on damask. In one room, tooled, gilded, and painted leather covers the walls beneath a gold and blue ceiling. The ceiling was made in Italy in the style of the sixteenth century, so that a large Venetian Renaissance painting could be set in it as it might have been in a salon on the Grand Canal. In the Raphael Room and the Titian Room, important paintings are hung near the windows for north light, and most

large paintings are above the wainscot, higher than the viewer's gaze. All of the galleries have furniture, and most have textiles on tables, behind pictures, or hung on the walls as works of art.

The collection includes four Rembrandts, a Rubens, and a Vermeer in the Dutch Room. The Tapestry Room displays three Spanish paintings together with the ten Flemish tapestries for which it was built. Three times a week concerts are held here, for music in the museum is a tradition. The Gothic Room, with its rough-hewn beams and dark panelling, has an interesting group of German wood sculpture mounted high up on the walls. Here Sargent's famous portrtait of Mrs. Gardner is placed at an angle near a window. It is one of a number of portraits of her, and is the best known, perhaps because it is often the last picture to be seen in the museum, but also because many are struck by its similarity to a medieval icon. Mrs. Gardner is present in the galleries in other ways: photographs and letters appear in cases along the way, and mixed with masterpieces are bits of her memorabilia as a constant reminder of personal associations, interests, and patronage. The breadth and extravagance of her experience fill every room almost to overflowing: a lifetime of travel and collecting arranged with care and devotion. Altogether there are almost 2,500 objects in thirty-two galleries. But it is the sum of the parts that is best remembered: rooms with a special character that has been imitated but never surpassed. These ideas for a museum are all the more interesting coming from a woman whose beginnings were not much different than many of her generation.

Isabella Stewart was born in New York on April 14, 1840, the oldest child of David and Adelia Smith Stewart, through whom she claimed Scottish descent from Robert Bruce on her father's side and colonial America on her mother's. In response to the snobbishness of Boston society, which thrived on family history, Isabella claimed that she and Mary, Queen of Scots were leaves on the same family tree. She grew up in New York City but passed many months with her grandmother on Long Island, which strengthened her character by association, and developed her instinct for country estates and gardening. Her father's business prospered and she and her brothers and sisters had governesses and tutors, and a life led in pleasant surroundings. At the age of sixteen her parents decided to take her to Europe to finish her education, and there,

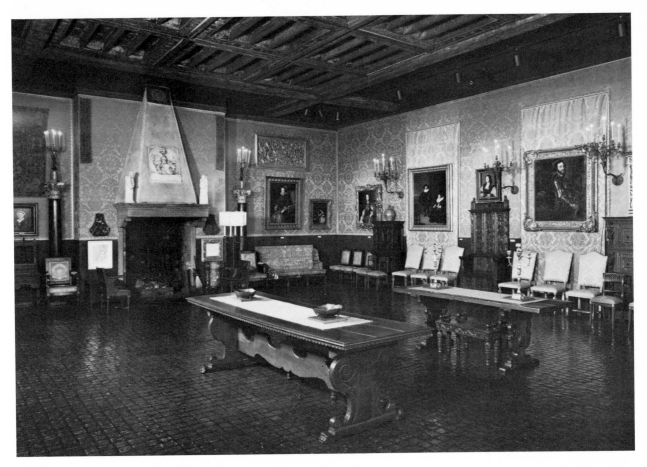

The Dutch Room

in a school in Paris, she met Julia Gardner, from Boston. From Paris the Stewarts proceeded to Rome, where they spent a number of weeks before going on to Venice, the city which became Isabella's second home and which would provide the inspiration for her dreams of a museum. They sailed for home toward the end of 1858.

Almost immediately upon her return to New York, Isabella accepted Julia Gardner's invitation to visit Boston. As Mr. Gardner was away on business, Julia wrote to him of the entertainments planned for her friend: dancing, singing, sleigh rides, dinner parties; in short, a world reminiscent of Currier and Ives arranged for her guest's delight. Isabella stayed long enough to receive a proposal from Julia's brother Jack, to which she responded, "If you want to ask that

question, you will have to come to New York." Jack, who had left Harvard after one year to join the family business, now had excellent prospects. In the words of Morris Carter, her first biographer, "the match was highly satisfactory to both families. Miss Stewart had wealth and charm; Mr. Gardner had wealth and position." By the end of February 1859, the couple were engaged and on April 12, 1860, two days before her twentieth birthday, Isabella was married. Throughout their married life, Jack kept a record of whatever they bought for the house, and their first entry was for two photographs purchased in New York on the way back from their honeymoon in Washington.

The young couple lived first with his father and then at a hotel until their house on Beacon Street, a present

Isabella Stewart Gardner

to distress her. After this, her strength and spirit never wavered until a crippling stroke late in life made her almost an invalid. From Norway and Sweden, she and her husband travelled to Russia, and came home seven months later by way of Vienna, where she renewed her passion for music, and Paris, where she found an interest in fashion. The change was soon noticed in Boston. "Quickly she became one of the most conspicuous members of Boston Society," writes Carter. "Effervescent, exuberant, reckless, witty, she did whatever she pleased, and the men, the gayest and most brilliant of them, she captivated." From that moment on, Mrs. Gardner became a personality and was given increasing attention by the press, until at the height of her success, she was reported with the same mixture of adulation and curiosity that later was associated with Hollywood. One reporter wrote in 1875: "Mrs. Jack Gardner is one of the seven wonders of Boston. There is nobody like her in any city in this country. She is a millionaire Bohemienne. She is eccentric, and she has the courage of eccentricity. She is the leader of the smart set, but she often leads where none dare follow. She is 35, plain and wide-mouthed, but has the handsomest neck, shoulders and arms in all Boston. She imitates nobody; everything she does is novel and original.... All Boston is divided into two parts, of which one follows science, and the other Mrs. Jack Gardner."

It is no wonder that Bernard Berenson referred to her as "Boston's pre-cinema star."

The next decade was marked as much by travel as by her life in society. The death in 1874 of Isabella's brother David, to whom she had been devoted, meant that she could not appear during the season in Boston. She and Jack decided to spend the winter in Egypt. Her trip up the Nile was recorded in a diary illustrated by her own charming watercolor drawings. After an exhausting journey through the Near East, the couple arrived in Athens in July, only to learn that Jack's older brother had died. Upon their return home, they became the guardians of three orphaned nephews, and Isabella finally had the pleasure of raising children and seeing to their education. On their next trip abroad the boys accompanied them on a pilgrimage to the cathedrals of England and France, with time out for the races at Ascot and the Oxford-Cambridge cricket match.

As the Gardners travelled, the house on Beacon

from Mr. Stewart, was completed. All was not bliss for the young bride, who was not in robust health and who often found the constraints of Boston society an unnecessary burden. Both the older Gardner boys had married after Jack and both had sons within a year or two, while Isabella remained childless. By 1862, they were in their own house and in a year the young couple rejoiced in the birth of a son. Just as they were pulling the threads of life together, the baby died. The blow was almost unbearable for the mother, who had been warned by the doctor that she could not have another child. Two years of depression and illness followed. The doctor suggested travel, and in 1867 she was taken by ambulance to a ship and carried aboard on a litter.

The change of scene had its effect, and by the time she reached Scandinavia, Isabella seemed recovered, although throughout her life the memory of her son remained

A party in the Music Room at 152 Beacon Street, ca. 1888.
Mrs. Gardner is on the right, Jack Gardner is standing.

Street began to take on an international flavor. The intent was still to furnish a home, but among its accoutrements were examples of nineteenth-century French paintings, prints, decorative panels, and bits of stained glass. In 1880, Mrs. Gardner bought a Corot and, before the year was out, had purchased the house next door. Now there was a proper music room for her private concerts and ample wall space for new acquisitions. She had come under the influence of Charles Eliot Norton, the first Professor of Fine Arts at Harvard, and attended his lectures. In the spring of 1885, he invited her to join the Dante Society, which met at his house. Before long, she was buying rare books with his encouragement, and throughout her life she added to that collection, although it soon became a secondary interest. Her friends included Boston's literary society: James Russell Lowell, Oliver Wendell Holmes, Julia Ward Howe, and, in 1881, the young writer F. Marion Crawford, Mrs. Howe's nephew. Together she and Craw-

Bernard Berenson

ford spent many hours reading Dante. He had grown up in Italy and was therefore an excellent tutor, and at twenty-eight he had just written his first novel, the manuscripts of which he gave to Isabella.

By 1883, the Gardners were ready for a trip around the world. Tales of the Orient had been brought to Boston by recent visitors and Mrs. Gardner was determined to learn about it at first hand. In May they sailed for Japan. A year later they arrived in Venice, having passed through China, Java, Cambodia, India, and Egypt. After the Orient, Venice held more than its usual charm for the visitors, both weary from strange lands and interminable travel. Venice meant friends, relatives, and familiar things. The Daniel Curtises, cousins of Jack, had bought the Palazzo Barbaro on the Grand Canal, and their son Ralph, himself a painter, offered to show them through Venice. Mrs. Gardner bought photographs of those things that impressed her most and later put them in scrapbooks for reference. Thereafter, every trip to Europe meant a trip to Venice, where she would rent the Palazzo Barbaro for months at a time, and where in 1897 and 1899 much of the architectural detail for the museum was purchased.

She was not yet a collector of art, but by 1886 she had met James Abbott McNeill Whistler in London, and was introduced to John Singer Sargent by her old friend Henry James. Whistler did a pastel of her, and she bought a second pastel and a small painting. In Sargent's studio she saw the famous portrait of Madame X, and began a friendship with the artist which was to last for the rest of her life. It was cemented the following year, when Sargent came to Boston and painted the portrait that dominates the Gothic Room in the museum.

Her patronage of contemporary artists, tentative though it was, may be considered Mrs. Gardner's beginning as an art collector. In Boston she much admired the work of Denis Bunker, who painted her portrait and gave her several of his canvases. He convinced her to buy a painting by Thomas Dewing, a painter much admired by Freer. Young musicians also received her help, and her influence on music in Boston, through her private concerts and encouragement of the new Symphony Orchestra, did much to shape the city's aspirations in the twentieth century.

Her other passion was horticulture. The Beacon Street house was filled with flowers. From the street they could be seen in a bay window over the front door; inside they were everywhere evident. When she and Jack inherited the Brookline estate from his parents, she set about to remake the gardens which became, in their way, as well known as her Paris gowns and jewelry. Because of her great interest in music, the tradition of concerts continues today in the same way that flowers from the museum's greenhouse continue to appear throughout the building.

In 1888, an Easter spent in Seville, with its religious services and festivals, inspired her to buy her first old master painting, a Madonna and Child by Zurbarán (now attributed to a close follower). With the death of her father in 1891, and an inheritance of nearly two million dollars, she was at last ready to embark on a career of serious collecting, and she did so with surprising acumen. Among the pictures she acquired were the Vermeer *Concert* and a Pesellino Madonna boldly bought at auctions in Paris and London. Shortly thereafter, through a remarkable stroke of luck, she began to receive the help and counsel of Bernard Berenson.

She had met Berenson when he was an undergraduate at Harvard, and had helped him by contributing substantially to a stipend raised by one of his professors

The Veronese Room

so that he might study abroad. In his letters to her of 1887–89, it is possible to follow his slow transformation from incipient writer to art connoisseur, and his commitment to Italy and the Renaissance. When he announced his intention to remain abroad, Mrs. Gardner ended the correspondence; but when, five years later, in 1894, the grateful scholar sent her his first book, *The Venetian Painters of the Renaissance*, she renewed the friendship and allowed him to act for her in purchasing works of art, in which pursuit he was no less eager than she. This was usually done by letter: a picture was described and a photograph enclosed with an estimated price of what he believed he could negotiate. Often he asked her to cable an answer. By 1896, his letters often spoke of "her Gallery,"

and indeed Jack and Isabella were talking of building a museum. The first plan was to tear down their adjoining houses on Beacon Street and erect a museum there.

The Gardners' acquisitions, which had become more frequent with the help of Berenson, were further accelerated by a trip they took in 1897. Not only paintings but marble balconies, columns, capitals and reliefs, furniture, tapestries, and sculpture were found for the museum, which was in the planning stage when they left. The buying continued through 1898, but during that year the plans for a museum took a decided turn. Jack argued for building on the newly reclaimed land in the Fens, where the museum could have a garden and windows on all four sides.

Unfortunately, Jack Gardner died suddenly on De-

The Gothic Room

cember 10, 1898. His constant pleasure in his wife's ambitions, and particularly in the collection, cannot be underestimated. In addition to his success in business, he had served since 1886 as Treasurer of the Boston Museum of Fine Arts and had managed Isabella's money for her with considerable tact. He left the bulk of his estate to his widow, including the right to invade capital if she so desired—an expression of his confidence in her.

Mrs. Gardner, disconsolate by her sudden loss, threw her energy into the creation of the museum. Ground was broken in 1899, and she returned to Europe in order to find more architectural elements for the structure now going up on the edge of the park in the westernmost section of the city. These joined the earlier purchases in a warehouse, waiting for the proper moment to be summoned by Mrs. Gardner. Upon her return, she spent every day on the job with the workmen, determined that nothing should be left to chance. The stairs were put in and taken out twice before the desired effect was achieved. The court walls were to be sponged to simulate marble, and this she demonstrated for the workmen by climbing a scaffold and dipping a sponge into a bucket of white paint, then one of pink. She fought with the building inspector and with the electric company, fired workmen summarily, and demanded that work stop when she wasn't there to supervise. The costs, if she ever considered them, were substantial, and when at last the building was completed, Mrs. Gardner realized that never again could she collect with such abandon, neither would she be able to live in the same luxury she had once enjoyed.

Fenway Court rose behind a huge brick wall which enclosed a garden. The street facade, a simple exterior in yellow brick, did little to satisfy public curiosity as to Mrs. Gardner's museum. One story had it that she had imported a palazzo from Florence which was being rebuilt on the site. A few friends did see the building after she took up residence there in December 1901, but another year was to pass, during which she arranged the collection, before the official opening.

On the night of January 1, 1903, guests entered a large music room in which, just after nine o'clock, fifty members of the Boston Symphony Orchestra played a Bach chorale with Lena Little among the nine singers from the Cecilia Society. This was followed by Mozart's overture to *The Magic Flute*, Chausson's symphonic poem *Viviane*, and Schumann's *Overture, Scherzo and Finale, Opus 52*. When the doors to the courtyard were rolled back, guests wandered under Japanese lanterns among the flowers in the court, and up the Venetian staircase into the rooms of the museum, lit with candles and *torchères* and with fires blazing in each fireplace. Mrs. Gardner's triumph was complete. Not only were friends generous in their praise, but press notices of the opening were universally warm, and compliments came from absent friends who had received word of it.

The public was admitted for the first time in February 1903 and thereafter was limited to 200 visitors a day for about a month each year. Nevertheless, Mrs. Gardner complained to Berenson of the duties thrust on her as a museum director. However, close friends were always ready to join her for dinner, or to organize concerts and other entertainments, and she continued to maintain the house in Brookline during warm weather; but the *belle époque* had passed.

When Berenson and his wife arrived in America in 1904, he was recognized everywhere as a great connoisseur of art, and was entertained extensively by collectors and museum directors, first and foremost among them, Mrs. Gardner. It was becoming evident to him that to maintain his life in his Florentine villa he would have to cultivate new patrons. Mrs. Gardner was spending less and would often rely on other experts for advice: Richard Norton in Rome, Sargent in London, and friends in Boston such as Denman Ross and Joseph Lindon Smith. Within a few years, Berenson became allied with the great dealer Duveen, but he continued to offer Mrs. Gardner first refusal on objects particularly suited to the museum, and pursued their long correspondence with warmth and candor.

Ten Flemish tapestries from circa 1550 were bought in 1910, and that perhaps was the deciding factor in Mrs. Gardner's decision to destroy the large music room and create more galleries—three on the ground floor and one above, the Tapestry Room, the floor of which divided the original space. America's entry into the World War further reduced Mrs. Gardner's ability to buy paintings. As the war ended, so too did her active life; in December 1919 she had a stroke. Although she could move around the museum, and enjoyed seeing close friends, and on occasion went out in a car, she no longer entertained or appeared in public. She died peacefully on July 17, 1924. For three days her coffin rested in the little chapel on the first floor, and under her instructions mass was said daily by priests from the Society of St. John the Evangelist. She was buried beside her husband and child in Mt. Auburn Cemetery, Cambridge.

Did that "dense splendid tissue of adventure," which James found in her life, lead her to the collection and this museum, or was it a childhood inspiration that guided Isabella throughout her remarkable course to its fulfillment? In a letter written to her not long before she died, a friend remembered what Italy had meant to her as a child: "I first met you taking my Italian lessons with you and Helen Waterston, do you remember it? I also remember what you said to me (you were about 16 years old) namely that if you ever inherit any money that it was yours to dispose of, you would have a house, a house like the one in Milan [the Poldi-Pezzoli Museum] filled with beautiful pictures & objects of Art, for people to come and enjoy. And you have carried out the dream of your youth & given great happiness to hundreds of people. And how grateful we are to you for it, dear Mrs. Gardner."

Rollin van N. Hadley,
Director

Plate List

The Courtyard

All the main rooms and stair halls of Fenway Court open onto the central courtyard, which is filled with flowers from the museum's greenhouse. Venetian window frames, balustrades, medallions, and fragments of stone reliefs are set into the walls, while the objects in the courtyard are mainly from the classical world. A fountain splashes by the far wall and a Roman mosaic pavement from the second century is at the center.

17

Paintings and Drawings

GIOTTO

b. Colle di Vespignano, ca. 1267
d. Florence, 1336/37

The Presentation of the Infant Jesus in the Temple

After 1320
Gold and tempera on panel
45.2 x 43.6 cm. (17 3/4 x 17 1/4 in.)
Acquired in 1900

Giotto was justly famous in his lifetime, immortalized by Petrarch and Dante, and by the monumental commissions of extraordinary power which he successfully completed. Despite its small size, *The Presentation in the Temple* is a cornerstone of the Gardner Museum, a splendid example of what the artist has meant in terms of Western painting. Comparison may be made within the museum with the altarpiece by Simone Martini, Giotto's famous contemporary (page 21), which has a format typical before Giotto's time and is an example of the Gothic international style of the period.

In Giotto we have the beginnings of realism. His figures not only behave in believable ways but have the weight and substance drawn from a knowledge of anatomy. This painting also shows his instinctive touch with tempera colors; he plays bright hues against a gold ground in such a way as to bring the actors into focus. The gesture of the Child reaching for his mother, the expression of Simeon the priest, whose eyes have seen the salvation, the concern evinced by Mary sharpen this moment of great religious significance. To either side of the central figures stand the priestess Anna holding the scroll with the ancient prophecy and Joseph carrying two pigeons, the traditional offering for the firstborn male.

The colors—pink, vermilion, orange, and chartreuse—characteristic of Giotto's late frescoes in Santa Croce in Florence, may be found in the other panels associated with this one. These are *The Epiphany*, in the Metropolitan Museum of Art, New York, *The Last Supper*, *The Crucifixion*, and *The Descent into Hell*, in the Alte Pinakothek, in Munich, *The Entombment* in the Berenson Collection at Settignano, and *The Pentecost*, in the London National Gallery.

Because the scenes are not oriented to move the eye from left to right and are almost square, unlike predella panels, various explanations have been put forward as to their original use, for example, as panels on a chest or sacristy door. They represent Giotto's mature style of the 1320s.

19

SIMONE MARTINI

b. Siena, 1283/85
d. Avignon, 1344

The Madonna and Child, With Four Saints

Ca. 1320
Tempera on panel
Dimensions excluding pinnacles:
  Central panel: 140 x 57 cm.
  (55 1/4 x 22 1/2 in.)
  Other panels: 121 x 39 cm.
  (47 1/2 x 15 1/2 in.)
Acquired 1899

Petrarch wrote, "I have known two painters of talent, one Giotto, in high reknown among the moderns, the other Simone of Siena." Indeed, Simone was the foremost painter of his age in a style that brought the Gothic influence of France to Italian painting. This polyptych, his only complete altarpiece outside of Italy, has the Madonna and Child with Saints Paul, Lucy, Catherine, and John the Baptist. The figures in the pinnacles, angels sounding the trumpets of the Last Judgement, angels with the instruments of Christ's Passion, and Christ displaying his wounds, have been used as evidence that the altarpiece was commissioned by the *Zelanti*, or conservative, Franciscan friars, who opposed more modern concepts within their order. It is thought that the altarpiece was made for the monastery church of San Francesco in Orvieto, the town where Simone had been employed, perhaps just before this, to do another altarpiece for the church of San Domenico in 1320.

After the museum acquired this polyptych, the paintings were transferred to new panels and new frames were substituted. In its original form, according to recent research, all five panels were joined together, with pier shafts rising above the pinnacles in place of the columns that now enframe each panel. Simone thus imposed an order and proportion on the complex, many-panelled altarpieces current at that time.

He was the master of forms in low relief, and the contours, drawn in pure colors that are echoed from panel to panel, are complex and refined, and often enhanced with subtle linear details, such as the line of St. Lucy's cloak or the curls on the Child's head. With this sensuous beauty, he influenced painters from Naples to Avignon for more than a century, and in his native city for even longer. None were able to surpass him, and the next leap forward was made not from Simone's aesthetics, but from the realism of Giotto.

LIPPO MEMMI

b. Siena, active 1317 (?)
d. Siena, 1347

The Madonna and Child

Tempera on panel
33.5 x 25.3 cm. (13 1/4 x 10 in.)
Acquired 1897

This portable altar shows all the loving care with which the artist-craftsman could enhance a spiritual work. It is in miniature form a reflection of the large altarpiece by Lippo's brother-in-law and mentor Simone Martini. The ornamentation is painstakingly applied to the raised arcade along the bottom and the halos and decorative borders, including the engaged frame. The decoration continues on the gilded reverse, which also has a pronounced border and raised frame. The figures along the bottom are St. Helen, St. Paul, St. Dominic—evidently the patron saint—St. Stephen, and a full-length figure of a praying nun, probably the donor and a member of a Dominican order.

Lippo's father was a painter, possibly Simone's master, and early in life Lippo was attached to Simone's shop. After the latter's departure for Avignon, Lippo accepted commissions on his own, and a number bear his signature. Although he never mastered the subtleties of the older artist, his sturdy figures in strong, massed colors have an immediate effect, conveying the devotion of the artist and the care and regard that he gave them with his unsparing labors.

23

MASACCIO

b. San Giovanni Valdarno, 1401
d. Rome, 1428/29

A Young Man in a Scarlet Turban

Ca. 1425–27
Tempera on panel
41 x 30 cm. (16 x 11 3/4 in.)
Acquired 1898

In less than twenty-eight years of life and with less than a decade in his active career, Masaccio realized a place in the history of painting exceeded by very few artists. He concerned himself with rendering figures in light and shade, and in his frescoes portrayed nature and man with a remarkable understanding of form built on modelled surfaces. Disdaining the hard outlines and flat colors that his contemporaries favored, he used a precise and directed light in his pictures, and his figures stand in comprehensible space within a geometric perspective.

There are two other Quattrocento profile portraits in the Gardner collection; this is the earliest of the three. They are among the few personal portraits that survive from the middle years of the fifteenth century in Italy, the first serious pictures not devoted to religious subjects. While portraits of donors sometimes appear as details in religious pictures, these personal objects are the precursors of all modern portrait painting.

The tunic and turban are contemporary, and may also be seen in Masaccio's frescoes in the Church of the Carmine, Florence; for example, the two men on the left in the scene of St. Peter baptizing are similarly dressed. The idea of the profile portrait may have been taken from the relief portraits that appeared on Roman coins, or that were painted in miniature in illuminated medieval manuscripts.

25

FRA ANGELICO

b. Vicchio, ca. 1390–95
d. Rome, 1455

The Dormition and the Assumption of the Virgin

Ca. 1430
Gold and tempera on panel
61.8 x 38.5 cm. (24 1/4 x 15 1/8 in.)
Acquired 1899

This small reliquary panel is one of a series of four painted between 1425 and 1430 for the Dominican church of Santa Maria Novella in Florence and used as principal decorations on the shrine altars during high religious festivals. The four panels depict scenes in the life of the Virgin; the Gardner panel falls third chronologically. The other three are in the former convent of San Marco in Florence, now the Fra Angelico museum.

Fra Angelico was a pious Dominican monk who was already well known by 1433 as a painter and illuminator. He painted in fresco as well as tempera, and always on religious themes. He worked for the last years of his life in Rome.

In the lower part of the panel, the death of the Virgin is depicted. Christ stands before the Virgin's bier in the center of a group of fourteen saints. He holds in his arms a small child, representing the Virgin's soul. St. Peter, in priest's vestments, reads the office, while two apostles act as attendant priests. St. John stands at the foot of the bier holding a spreading palm, symbolizing Mary's triumph over death. Four other disciples place the bier in position, their hands still on the carrying poles. Although the group is large, the character and attitude of each face is clearly defined.

The middle of the panel represents the Assumption of the Virgin. In a wreath of golden light Mary rises, half standing, half floating on the clouds, some of which blow across the sweeping folds of her robes. There is a swirl of attendant angels at her sides and below, and six angels playing instruments float lightly and gracefully around her head. The detail of the angels' robes, painted in light colors and gilded, is skillfully rendered, as are their individual gestures and facial expressions. In the upper part of the panel Christ, surrounded by cherubim, extends his hands to receive the Virgin.

The middle section of the panel in particular shows the finest qualities of Angelico's early works. His use of color is rich and fresh, with a resulting sense of atmosphere as the essence of light and air. His skill in rendering movement is everywhere evident in this central scene. In the overall composition Angelico shows a mastery not evident in his earlier works, in which linear design is often stiff and formal with faces somewhat caricatured. Here the composition is harmonious and rhythmical.

27

PESELLINO

b. Florence (?), 1422
d. Florence, 1457

The Madonna and Child with a Swallow

Ca. 1440–50
Tempera on panel
59.7 x 39.5 cm. (23 1/2 x 15 1/2 in.)
Acquired 1892

Bought at auction by Mrs. Gardner herself, this painting came with the attribution to Fra Filippo Lippi. A close relationship existed between the two artists: Lippi's altarpiece for Santa Croce (now in the Uffizi) has a predella by Pesellino, perhaps his earliest work. Pesellino's style was formed by his association with Lippi and also by the example of Fra Angelico, from which he developed, in his short lifetime, a vocabulary all his own. The Gardner panel is a good example of the private altarpiece of the mid-fifteenth century, embodying all the advances made by the first generation of the Renaissance. The style and mood presented here would reach its culmination in the work of Botticelli twenty-five years later.

The popularity of this panel can be judged by the number of surviving copies, often with a different background, both from Pesellino's hand and by other associates of lesser reputation. In our version, the Madonna was placed in front of a marble niche and the Child holds a barn swallow, a symbol of the Resurrection.

Berenson was among the first to recognize Pesellino's talent, and five years after the acquisition of this panel was able to offer Mrs. Gardner two *cassoni* panels by the same artist, which remain in the collection of the museum.

29

ATTRIBUTED TO
PAOLO UCCELLO

b. Florence, 1397
d. Florence, 1475

A Young Lady of Fashion

After 1450
Oil (?) on panel
44 x 32 cm. (17 3/8 x 12 1/2 in.)
Acquired 1914

The young lady is dressed expensively. Her dress, tailored to button at the shoulder, shows a rich damask at the sleeve. Her necklace of pearls and blue stones ends with a circular red pendant. The carefully brushed hair carries another set of pearls at the back, and is held in place with a cap decorated with more jewels. In keeping with the prevailing style, she has an artificially high forehead emphasized by a string of beads. The background was once azurite blue, of which traces may still be seen, and there are worn places, notably the blue dress and the space between the eye and eyebrow. Nevertheless, the fundamental quality of the panel remains, and there is about it a sense of design and presence which suggests the work of a master. The present attribution has never been universally accepted and the only certainty is that another profile picture of a lady in the Metropolitan Museum of Art, New York, is by the same hand. Both these works date from shortly after the middle of the fifteenth century, and are considered Florentine, but were not necessarily painted from life. An artist known only as the Master of the Castello Nativity is now considered by several critics to be the author of both panels.

Like the Masaccio (see page 25), it represents the beginnings of portrait painting as secular art in the Renaissance. The artist's preoccupation with decorative elements and the strong outlines are contrasted with the softer flesh tones, while the rigid pose with its elongated neck produces an aesthetic, more than a naturalistic, vision of femininity.

PIERO DELLA FRANCESCA

b. Borgo San Sepolcro, ca. 1416
d. Borgo San Sepolcro, 1492

Hercules

Ca. 1465–70
Fresco
151 x 126 cm. (59 1/4 x 49 1/2 in.)
Acquired 1906

By 1439, Piero was at work in Florence with Domenico Veneziano and had already assimilated the style of the Florentine Renaissance. Throughout his long, active life he travelled in northern and central Italy and perhaps more than any other artist was responsible for spreading Florentine style beyond Tuscany. Although his panel paintings survive in a number of museums, including in his home town, his monument is his great cycle of frescoes for San Francesco in Arezzo.

The fresco in the museum is Piero's only pagan subject and is further evidence of his interest in rendering anatomy. His figures are seldom active, rather his success came from his clear compositions and careful modelling, always painted with studied proportions and a calculated use of light. There is a gravity about his pictures and a majestic quality, gained perhaps from a knowledge of the classical world.

The fresco was found in a house in Borgo San Sepolcro, presumably occupied at one time by the artist. Hercules, with his club and lion's skin, is painted to be seen from below and with that in mind the background may be interpreted as a timbered ceiling and the enframement, a window. A close examination reveals the perforation used when the original drawing was transferred to the plaster.

Renaissance artists usually painted architectural decoration of this kind with several figures. Castagno's decoration of the Villa Carducci Pandolfini at Legnaia, for example, has a series of famous men from history or mythology painted as though standing in the openings of the portico. Unfortunately, this figure is the only portion of the wall to survive and there is no document recording the extent of Piero's decoration in the house. The fresco is usually dated in the 1460s, either during or just after the work in Arezzo.

33

BARTOLOMÉ BERMEJO

b. Córdoba, Spain, 1436/39
d. After 1498, place unknown

St. Engracia

Ca. 1474
Gold and oil on panel
164 x 73 cm. (64 9/16 x 28 3/4 in.)
Acquired 1904

Although Bermejo holds an important place in the history of Spanish painting of the fifteenth century, his oeuvre is small and represented by only four pictures in this country. He no doubt learned his technique from a Netherlandish painter, and is thought to have travelled to Flanders at one time. This painting was considered Netherlandish when it appeared at auction in Brussels in 1904.

This is the central panel from a large altarpiece with a predella of four saints and a scene of *The Resurrection*, and a central pinnacle of *The Crucifixion*. These are in Daroca, near Saragossa, and recent documents indicate that the altarpiece was painted there between 1474 and 1477. Three additional panels with scenes of the life of the saint survive: *The Arrest*, in San Diego, California, *The Flagellation*, in Bilbao, Spain, and *The Imprisonment*, in Daroca. These, with at least one more, would have been placed on either side of the Gardner panel.

St. Engracia holds the palm of the Virgin Martyr, and the nail with which she was killed. She sits on a wooden throne inlaid with simple decoration, dressed in robes embellished with ermine and pearls. The artist has included a favorite motif: a transparent veil. It falls from her head to encircle her neck and swirls to the right, balancing the heavy crown which is slightly to the left. The inscription on her shoe may be purely decorative, as no interpretation for the lettering has been suggested.

According to legend, St. Engracia, a Portuguese princess, passed through Saragossa with her retinue on her way to meet her fiancé, the Duke of Roussillon. She was arrested, tortured, and finally killed for denouncing the treatment of Christians by the Roman Proconsul. Centuries later, the discovery of her body, followed by miraculous cures attached to its presence, caused her veneration among the local population, although her story was little known elsewhere.

35

CARLO CRIVELLI

b. Venice, 1430/35
d. The Marches, 1495

St. George and the Dragon

1470
Gold and tempera on poplar wood
94 x 47.8 cm. (37 x 18 $^{13}/_{16}$ in.)
Acquired 1897

"You never in your life have seen anything so beautiful for color, and in line it is drawn as if by lightning," Berenson wrote Mrs. Gardner in 1897. Later he wrote, "It is the only one I shall envy you. The others may be greater, but this one I love the most." The painting he refers to is from a large, many-panelled altarpiece which was removed from its original location and broken up following the demolition of the parish church at Porto San Giorgio on the Adriatic. This panel of St. George is the gem of the polyptych. The central panel with the Madonna and Child, now in the National Gallery, Washington, includes a minute figure of the donor, one Giorgio Salvadori, an Albanian who like the church and the port town, had St. George as his patron saint. For that reason the artist lavished all his skills on this, which was to the right of the Madonna and Child. The other panels are two standing saints, now in the National Gallery, London, a large lunette with the Entombment, now in Detroit, and smaller lunettes which stood over the side panels, each with two half-length figures of saints, now in Tulsa and Cracow.

The handsome, youthful St. George, the epitome of the Renaissance ideal, is placed in a setting that draws heavily on the Gothic painters of Northern Italy, particularly Venice, where Crivelli began his career. He left that city at the moment when Giovanni Bellini was transforming her art, and passed most of his remaining years in the more isolated climate of the Marches. The spiky landscape, with its miniature medieval town and formal garden, is presented with the same care as the foreground, with its armored rider, his rearing horse, and the reptilian dragon. The decorative patterns—the horse's harness and the saint's garments and halo—are embossed and heightened with gold, which is also used to cover the sky. Although part of a larger work, this painting, entirely balanced and self-contained, stands better on its own, where it may be appreciated as one of the finest examples of the artist's work.

37

GIOVANNI DI PAOLO

Active in Siena after 1472
d. Siena, 1482/3

The Child Jesus Disputing in the Temple

Ca. 1472
Tempera transferred to linen on panel
27.5 x 23.9 cm. (10 $\frac{13}{16}$ x 9 $\frac{3}{8}$ in.)
Acquired 1908

Siena fell far behind Florence in the advances made in realistic painting during Giovanni's long career, which never wavered in its dedication to the style that had made his city famous. She continued, through the fifteenth century, to be a center of art and commerce, and to foster famous men, notably Pope Pius II. Giovanni painted in tempera, relying heavily on the masters of the previous century, with only occasional signs of his knowledge of the more vibrant work which was transforming the art of Florence. He is at his best in small panels such as this or in manuscript illuminations, a number of which survive.

In this panel, the seated Doctors occupy a cramped space surrounding Christ, traditionally a boy of twelve, whose significance is further enhanced by his large size in this picture. Despite its unnatural proportions, the story is still clearly told, and the setting and the action are given a charming individualism. Christ appears to be in the middle of an argument that engages the Doctors' rapt attention. The figure on the left has guided Joseph and Mary to him, the former in bewilderment, the latter in amazement at discovering the group. They help to break up the rigid symmetry of the architecture further unbalanced by the play of bright colors, which give life to an otherwise static and grey composition.

Two other panels of similar size have been associated with this painting, suggesting that they once formed a part of a predella. *The Nativity*, in the Fogg Art Museum, Harvard, and *The Adoration of the Magi* in a private New York collection, take place out of doors, with a terraced hill in the background and the figures in front of a stable. Because of the symmetry of the scene in the temple, it logically falls in the center of a predella, which would have included other scenes from the life of Christ.

39

GENTILE BELLINI

b. Venice, 1429
d. Venice, 1507

A Turkish Artist

Ca. 1479–80
Pen and gouache on parchment
18 x 14 cm. (7 1/4 x 5 1/2 in.)
Acquired 1907

Older brother to the greatest Venetian painter of the fifteenth century, and brother-in-law to Mantegna, Gentile Bellini was never blessed with their genius, either in the presentation of large themes or in the selection of colors to carry them out. His large canvases of the pageants of his native city are remembered more for the accuracy of detail than for their sense of space and movement. He is best in his dignified portraits of Venetian nobility, painted in half-length and often in profile.

This unusual portrait was in an album purchased from a Turkish family early in this century. General agreement among critics connects the work with the Venice of the late fifteenth century, since Turkish painting of the period, exemplified by a version of this painting in the Freer Gallery, Washington, lacks the shading or rounded forms seen here. The attribution to Bellini rests on two points: the first, which is certain, is that the Doge of Venice, at the request of the Sultan Mohammed II, sent Gentile to Constantinople in 1479, where he worked for more than a year; the second, which is hypothetical, is that the inscription could be translated through Greek and with substitutions for sounds to contain the name Bellini. Despite these tenuous links, the painting has been attributed to Gentile by a number of authorities.

Whatever the facts, the work is a fascinating and rare object, combining delightful elements of East and West, and immensely decorative in its coloring as well as its patterns. The sumptuous costume implies a man of means, a noble who has turned his hand to painting. It is likely that the painting, if indeed done by Bellini, was later inscribed by a Turkish artist, who may then have added the border and the flower on the wall.

COSIMO TURA

b. Ferrara (?), ca. 1430
d. Ferrara, 1495

The Circumcision

Ca. 1470
Tempera and oil (?) on panel
39.1 x 38.2 cm. (15 1/4 x 15 in.)
Acquired 1901

The court at Ferrara under the house of Este demanded much of her artists, who were kept busy designing entertainments, personal bibelots, furniture, and textiles, as well as portraits and religious images. Tura is recorded there in 1451 and continued working in the city for almost forty years, as court painter to Duke Borso d'Este, and later for his brother, Ercole.

Tura's singular style emerged from the melding of old and new in the crosscurrents of Padua, where most probably he was apprenticed, and from the presence in Ferrara at mid-century, of Piero della Francesca and Roger van der Weyden. From these disparate elements, Tura evolved his own mannered and imaginative interpretation of religious and allegorical subjects, often inspired by the humanists and astrologers who dominated court life.

The Circumcision became a popular subject in the fifteenth century, although it is barely mentioned in the Bible. Simeon the priest and Mary are seated, Joseph holds a candle, and Anna stands ready to assist. These are the same figures that appear in the panel by Giotto in the Gardner collection (see page 19), but here the temple interior is suggested by an altar, on which rests a vase-like plaque with Moses praying to God the Father above. The plaque on the altar also appears with Hebraic writing in Tura's large panel of the *Madonna and Child* in the National Gallery, London, once the center of a large altarpiece.

There are two panels of the same shape: *The Adoration of the Magi* in the Fogg Museum, Harvard, and *The Flight into Egypt* in the Metropolitan Museum of Art, New York. Exactly how and where these panels were used has never been satisfactorily determined; as they are not the usual shape for parts of an altarpiece, they may have appeared on a piece of ecclesiastical furniture or a baptismal font.

43

MASTER OF THE GARDNER ANNUNCIATION

Umbrian

The Gardner Annunciation

Ca. 1480
Tempera with glazes, transferred
   to panel
102.4 x 114.8 cm. (40 3/8 x 45 3/16 in.)
Acquired 1900

The story of the Annunciation, always a favorite subject in Christian art, is beautifully presented here with a late fifteenth-century setting. The Renaissance villa, with its vaulted ceilings and tiled floor, has not changed the ancient concept in which the archangel Gabriel appears with a lily to announce his message to the Virgin at prayer. The Holy Ghost, represented by a dove, descends on a shaft of light. Beyond the garden door the artist has painted a landscape, a river flowing toward distant hills, and, at the point of geometric perspective, a tree—perhaps the Tree of Wisdom, for the painting, in keeping with the age, has symbolic overtones in much of the apparently casual detail.

The author of this classic example of fifteenth-century design was called by Berenson "the Master of the Gardner Annunciation." Various artists have been suggested, none universally accepted, but recent evidence has produced the name of an obscure painter from Umbria, Piermatteo da Amelia. This *Annunciation* comes from Assisi, and the artist was no doubt aware of Piero della Francesca's altarpiece painted not long before this for a convent in nearby Perugia. In Piero's *Annunciation*, a long cloister stretches back between the two figures and the Madonna is placed under the portico to the right. The points of similarity between the two paintings are many, in particular the use of the architecture to unify and enlarge the story.

The influence of recent Florentine painters, such as Verrocchio, can also be seen in the treatment of the figures themselves. Another possible author, under whose name the panel has appeared in the museum's catalogue, is Antoniazzo Romano, a prolific painter who worked primarily in Rome, often with more famous artists. The *Annunciation*, therefore, will continue to attract interest and research for some time to come.

45

SANDRO BOTTICELLI

b. Florence, 1444/45
d. Florence, 1510

The Madonna of the Eucharist

1470–74
Tempera on panel
85 x 64.5 cm. (33 1/2 x 25 3/8 in.)
Acquired 1899

Botticelli, more than any other artist, was the painter of the Florentine fifteenth century. His life spanned the golden age of Lorenzo de'Medici, and he had the misfortune to live on after the expulsion of Lorenzo's son, to see the sack of the Medici palace and Lorenzo's library, and the execution of Savanarola. His early training was with Filippo Lippi (whose son became Botticelli's student), but his inclination was toward the sculptural line and sensuous colors brought to refinement by his contemporaries Andrea del Verrocchio and Antonio del Pollaiuolo, both sculptors as well as painters. Neither was as prolific a painter as Botticelli, who accepted commissions for altarpieces, fresco decoration, and portraits. His talent extended to engravings (see page 149) and mosaic design but not to architecture or sculpture.

The twelve stalks of corn and the grapes represent the Eucharist, and by extension, the fruit of Christ's Passion, blessed by the Child and accepted by the Virgin as mediatrix between her Son and Man. The setting is a walled garden, beyond which one may see a landscape with a church and a tower, separated by a wandering stream. The singular physical beauty of the Madonna, Child, and angel, whose face is not an ethereal type but modelled with a sensual individuality never repeated in Botticelli's oeuvre, is remarkable in such an early work. Were it not for the rich colors on the right, and the more muted costume of the angel, the emphasis on the main figures would be lost in the wealth of details. But the luminous flesh tones combine with a sure sense of sculptural outline in the *Madonna and Child* to produce an imposing presence, totally religious as well as aesthetic.

47

SANDRO BOTTICELLI

The Tragedy of Lucretia

Ca. 1505
Tempera (?) and oil on panel
83.5 x 180 cm. (32 3/4 x 70 7/8 in.)
Acquired 1894

The story of Lucretia is told by Livy and Ovid, and she appears in Dante's *Inferno*. Tarquinius Sextus, son of the tyrant king of Rome, was so inflamed by her beauty and virtue that he raped her. The next day she called her father and her husband, who came with Lucius Junius Brutus. After telling them of her dishonor and extracting a promise of revenge, she committed suicide by plunging a dagger into her breast.

The attack by Tarquinius and Lucretia's suicide are shown in the arcades to the right and left of the panel, the center being given to the oath of vengeance proclaimed by Brutus over her body, witnessed by the citizens rushing to see what has happened. This oath resulted in the expulsion and death of the tyrant and his son, and led to the founding of the Republic of Rome, with Brutus as one of the two men entrusted with the powers of state.

The setting is classical in the foreground, with Italian and Flemish contemporary buildings behind, and a Tuscan landscape, and possibly Florentine battlements in the distance. Botticelli relies on the melodramatic gestures to convey the sense of activity and the greater sense of tragedy, which remains in sharp contrast to the serene setting. The decoration on the classical architecture includes scenes from the story of Judith and Holofernes to the left, as well as from Roman legends, and the figure of David with the head of Goliath on the column. Both Judith and David were heroes of Florence and are recalled here as further examples, beyond the central story of Lucretia, of tyrannicide. The painting can therefore be understood as a comment on the overthrow of the Medici government and the establishment of the citizens' government that ruled in Florence from 1494 to 1512. There is a companion piece to this panel, the *Story of Virginia* (now in the Accademia Carrara, Bergamo). The sacrifice of Virginia resulted in the restoration of the Roman Republic, much as Lucretia's martyrdom first established it. Both paintings may be dated after 1495, and a date of after 1500 seems most likely.

49

VITTORE CARPACCIO

b. Venice, 1460/65
d. Venice, ca. 1526

A Gondolier

Ca. 1494
Sepia with white gouache on blue
    paper
26 x 15 cm. (10 $\frac{1}{4}$ x 5 $\frac{7}{8}$ in.)
Acquired 1902

This drawing is related to a similar figure in the large painting entitled *The Healing of a Madman, with a View of the Rialto*, one of eight pictures commissioned by the Scuola di San Giovanni Evangelista, Venice, and now in the Accademia there. The eight pictures depict *The Legend of the True Cross*, and were painted by five leading Venetian artists in the last decade of the fifteenth century. These pictures embodied events of recent history and are peopled with portraits of Venetian citizens and views of the city itself. In Carpaccio's canvas for the series, the Rialto bridge (then made of wood) is in the background with numerous gondolas in front of it and a large crowd along the canal.

This particular gondolier is in the middle distance and his costume in the finished painting is more elaborate, with large white buttons running down the front of his coat, and black ribbons like those on the sleeves around the buttons. In place of a cap, the artist substituted a colorful headband with a large feather tucked into it. In the painting his red pants are painted with vertical white stripes to the knees, and his pole extends into the water. Another gondolier from this painting appears on a study sheet in Vienna. On the reverse of the Gardner drawing is a sketch of a man's head, probably from a later date, which has caused some critics to consider that the drawing was done after the painting, rather than for it.

50

ANDREA MANTEGNA

b. Isola di Carturo (?) ca. 1430
d. Mantua, 1506

Sacra Conversazione

Ca. 1495
Tempera on panel
53.5 x 42.8 cm. (21 x 16 3/4 in.)
Acquired 1899

This small painting, about the same size as the Fra Angelico (page 27), is, like that, filled with figures. The Fra Angelico is divided strictly between an upper and a lower register, while in this panel the foreground relates one story and the background is filled with scenes from the lives of the saints. The Virgin and Child are at the center of a gathering of seven holy women in a landscape, Saints Elizabeth and Mary Magdalen among them. John the Baptist is offering what appears to be a pomegranate to Christ. The landscape reveals a number of important events in the lives of the saints. St. Christopher carries the Child across the river; St. George is charging the dragon on the far shore. Ascending the mountain, the viewer sees St. Peter Martyr being assassinated, St. Jerome chastising himself before the crucifix, and St. Francis receiving the stigmata. On the horizon is that idealized city which appears in other works by the artist; is it Rome, Jerusalem or Constantinople?

Virgin, Child, and saints seated in the country was a subject imported to Italy from Northern Europe, and there christened as the *Sacra Conversazione*. This example was painted late in the artist's life, probably not before 1495. After his early training in Padua, Mantegna went as court painter to the Gonzagas in Mantua, where his long and significant career had its effect on the artists of Northern Italy and, through his brother-in-law Giovanni Bellini, on the art of Venice.

STUDIO OF
GIOVANNI BELLINI

Christ Bearing the Cross

Ca. 1505
Oil and tempera on panel
52.9 x 42.3 cm. (20 3/4 x 16 1/2 in.)
Acquired 1898

This was bought by Berenson as the work of Giorgione (and therefore a rare panel, indeed) from a noble house in Vicenza, at which time a will bequeathing it to the town was broken by the owner. A painting of the same subject by Giovanni Bellini, Giorgione's master, was discovered in 1939 and is now in Toledo, Ohio. In the Toledo picture, Christ's eyes are downcast, conveying the tragedy of the scene. In the painting shown here, the artist has changed the effect considerably: Christ engages the viewer directly. Some critics believe that both are by Bellini, while others consider the museum's panel an early, perhaps the earliest, work of Giorgione.

The artist has concentrated his efforts in this version in painting the face, done with an oil medium, while the costume and background were quickly brushed in with tempera. The subject was more popular in Northern Europe than in Italy, and was imported to the Veneto, where a third version of this painting remains today at Rovigo.

RAPHAEL

b. Urbino, 1483
d. Rome, 1520

Pietà

1503–06
Oil on panel
23.5 x 28.8 cm. (9 1/4 x 11 3/8 in.)
Acquired 1900

In its original location in the church of San Antonio at Perugia, this small predella panel was part of a large altarpiece commissioned between 1503 and 1506; the main panel and lunette are now in the Metropolitan Museum, New York, along with *The Agony in the Garden*, a panel the size of this one. Between them in the predella was a long panel of the *Procession to Calvary*, in the National Gallery, London, and on either end two standing saints now in the Dulwich Gallery near London.

Raphael was the pupil of Pietro Perugino, and the younger artist had his training in Perugia until he moved to Florence in 1504. This altarpiece is among his earliest commissions and his style is still close to that of his master, particularly in the dramatically posed figures of Nicodemus and Joseph of Arimathea. St. John's is a face that would appear again in Raphael's paintings, and may be compared with the head of the man directly behind the Pope's chair in the drawing on the following page.

The eye is led from the lower right upward to the left in the *Pietà*, the reverse of the arrangement in *The Agony in the Garden*. This structure provided the viewer with both symmetry and direction as he gazed at the altarpiece in its entirety. In the body of Christ, Raphael shows his growing sensitivity and maturity in the way the figure is modelled. Although his colors would later become more subtle and harmonious, this composition already shows his understanding of space and narrative. These traits developed in his short lifetime to make him the foremost painter of the High Renaissance in Rome.

RAPHAEL

Count Tommaso Inghirami

1511–12
Oil on panel
89.7 x 62.2 cm. (35 3/8 x 24 1/2 in.)
Acquired 1898

Raphael went to Rome in 1508 to paint the *Stanze* in the Vatican Palace for which he is best remembered. Although he continued to work on them for the rest of his life, with the ascendency of Leo X he became the architect of the new St. Peter's and then superintendent of excavations. Throughout, he was also a prolific portrait painter, particularly of the papal court, of which Tommaso Inghirami, secretary of the Lateran Council and Vatican Librarian, was an important figure.

Tommaso is seen here in scarlet cloth, perhaps to recall his service to the Lateran Council, and seated at his writing desk as an indication of his professed calling as a man of letters. Unfortunately little of his criticism of the classics ever reached print, yet he is remembered for his correspondence and as an actor, producer, and, in at least one instance, set designer for papal entertainments. As librarian, he was successful in adding important collections to the Vatican inventory.

Raphael has been true to his sitter, whose considerable girth and wall-eye were too well known to be overlooked. By turning the body and directing his glance away from the viewer, he has made him presentable and more interesting, so much so that this has been called the first portrait not self-contained, that is, presented as though the sitter were engaged with another person "off stage."

The painting came from the family palazzo in Volterra, where Lorenzo de'Medici had met Tommaso and adopted him after the death of his father. His advancement in the church was swift. As Papal Nuncio to the Emperor Maximilian, his success was so great that he returned with the titles Poet Laureate and Count Palatine. His death came following an accident in the Forum, in which he was thrown from his mount and suffered internal injuries. This was recorded by a votive panel now in the church of St. John Lateran in Rome. Another, slightly different version of the Raphael portrait is in the Pitti Palace in Florence.

59

ATTRIBUTED TO RAPHAEL

A Papal Procession

Ca. 1519
Chalk on paper
39.8 x 40.4 cm. (15 5/8 x 15 7/8 in.)
Acquired 1902

The commission to decorate a fourth room in the Vatican was given by the Medici Pope Leo X to Raphael in 1517, but at the time of Raphael's death work on the fresco had not yet begun. It was carried out after his death under the direction of his assistant, Giulio Romano. A drawing by Giulio, half of which is in the Rijksmuseum, Amsterdam, and the other half in the Nationalmuseum, Stockholm, is a further development of the scene presented here. In it the Pope is carried in a sedan chair and the mace bearer and the crucifix bearer are versions of the two figures in the Gardner drawing.

Here, the figure in the *Sedia Gestatoria* (an exclusively papal means of conveyance) wears a mitre instead of the papal tiara, identifying him as Sylvester I, Pope from 314–35, and the drawings as preparatory sketches for the fourth *Stanza*, called the *Sala di Costantino*.

Constantine, first Christian Roman Emperor (307–37), allowed the Bishop of Rome (the Pope) the privilege of wearing a diadem of gold set with jewels, but Sylvester chose to wear a white mitre, believing it more suitable for a person dedicated to religion. In the *Sala di Costantino*, one wall is decorated with a fresco depicting the *Donation of Constantine*, in which the Emperor, on his knees before the papal throne, makes the donation, a document giving the papacy temporal power over all of Italy and the West. The document was never universally accepted and was challenged as spurious in the fifteenth century. The papacy continued to defend it and at the time of the decorations of the *Stanze*, the Pope was extremely anxious to use the weight of the document to assert his authority over the Emperor of the Holy Roman Empire. The drawings in Stockholm and Amsterdam show Constantine's followers arriving on the right, and the Emperor at the head of his retinue falling on his knees before the advancing papal procession.

As Raphael prepared the designs for the *Stanze*, his drawings often show changes, seen here in the way the chair has been drawn over the figure below it. The use of colored chalks is without parallel in his sketches for the Vatican but an example of his work in chalk exists in the collection in Wilton House, Salisbury, Wiltshire.

Work on the *Sala di Costantino* was interrupted by the death of Leo X in 1522, but began again in 1524 and was essentially completed by August of that year. Leo's cousin, Clement VII, the Pope at this time, substituted his portrait for that of Sylvester in the fresco. In the drawing the face is that of Leo X.

60

61

PARIS BORDONE

b. Treviso, ca. 1500
d. Venice, 1571

The Child Jesus Disputing in the Temple

Ca. 1545
Oil on canvas
163 x 229 cm. (64 $\frac{1}{4}$ x 90 $\frac{1}{4}$ in.)
Acquired 1901

Christ and the Virgin balance the composition, picked out by the fall of light which draws our attention to their complementary gestures. The Child is disputing with one of the Doctors of the Temple, while a second, back to the viewer, tries to intercede. Another group in the center is concerned with the scriptures, while on the periphery various men with no apparent connection to the scene fill the voids. The room is alive with decorative touches, from the marble floor to the rich figures along the wall to carved capitals, steps, and turned railings. With loving care, the artist has left an ink pot, books, and scrolls strewn on the floor.

The classical symmetry and simplicity of early Renaissance taste have given way to a vocabulary of emotions, more human than devout, and more in keeping with the prosperous, febrile world of the Venetian Republic. This is the same story, very differently conceived, that Giovanni di Paolo depicted in about 1470 (see page 39), but in the span of time between the two paintings the scene has become one of operatic dimensions and the hall an adjunct to a contemporary basilica.

The dexterity that allowed Bordone to imbue his figures with a restless energy and place them in vast settings was never quite powerful enough to place him in the first rank of his profession. He borrowed heavily from others, but in time developed his own eccentric way of organizing narratives within a unified space.

In his youth, Bordone was in Titian's studio briefly, but very soon found the experience oppressive. Most of his work in the next decades was outside of Venice, in the Veneto, Lombardy, and, eventually, France and Germany. *The Child Jesus Disputing in the Temple* was painted on his return to Venice and passages seem to be directly borrowed from a painting of the same subject by Tintoretto, dated 1542–43. Large canvases such as this one soon lined the walls of Italian churches, their numbers increasing during the next two hundred years. They became so plentiful that, like the earlier gold-ground paintings, many were later sold and found their way into museums in Europe and America. This is the only example of its kind in Fenway Court, coming as it does from the first generation of painters to capitalize on the demand. Later examples from the Baroque masters had no appeal for collectors in the nineteenth century, and Italian painting after Titian, with few exceptions, was unknown in American collections.

MICHELANGELO

b. Caprese, 1475
d. Rome, 1564

Pietà

Ca. 1540–44
Black chalk on laid paper
29 x 19 cm. (11 3/8 x 7 1/2 in.)
Acquired 1902

This design employs two popular subjects, the Pietà, with the limp body of Christ between his mother's knees, and Christ supported by angels in the Tomb. The figures are in a tight hexagonal form, with Christ's head as the center. A sense of movement is generated by the angels, the upraised arms of the Virgin, and the weight of Christ's body, all pulling away from the center. The two central figures form a cross in front of the actual cross, which, before the sheet was cut at the top, ended in the shape of a "Y."

There is an engraving after the drawing dated 1546 as well as at least twelve other copies in various media. The drawing itself is dated between the years 1540 and 1544, after Michelangelo had completed the *Last Judgment* in the Sistine Chapel.

It is generally accepted as one of the presents that Michelangelo sent to Vittoria Colonna, described in Vasari's *Lives* (1568 edition) and in Condivi's biography of the artist as a dead Christ between the knees of the Virgin and supported by two angels. Vittoria Colonna (1490–1547) had profound influence on Michelangelo, evident in his art and expressed in the sonnets and letters he addressed to her. Widowed and living in a convent, she was active in an intellectual circle which included several cardinals bent on strict reform of the Church. Her piety was a source of inspiration to the artist, who recorded his great sorrow on hearing of her death.

Michelangelo carved his first Pietà when he was twenty-four years old, the marble now in St. Peter's. Because the subject embodies the highest aspirations of love and faith, he returned to it later, but was unable to finish either of the two versions begun in the last years of his life. One of these is the group in the Cathedral in Florence, a modification of the present arrangement, with Christ supported by the Virgin and Mary Magdalen. Nicodemus, who is above and behind the figure, is a self-portrait of the artist, who planned the Pietà for his own tomb.

65

BRONZINO

b. Monticelli, 1503
d. Florence, 1572

Study for a Figure in the Altarpiece of the Resurrection

Ca. 1549–1552
Black chalk on white paper
27.4 x 40.2 cm. (10 3/4 x 15 7/8 in.)
Acquired 1902

This drawing belonged at one time to Sir Joshua Reynolds and was bought from the Robinson Sale where, in 1902, Mrs. Gardner acquired most of her old master drawings. Robinson, a noted connoisseur and scholar, was the first director of what is now the Victoria and Albert Museum before his appointment as surveyor of the Queen's Collection. In his sale the drawing was listed as Michelangelo's study for Jonah on the Sistine Ceiling—an indication of the quality of the work.

It was identified not long ago as a study by Bronzino for his altarpiece in the Guadagni Chapel, Church of the Santissima Annunziata, Florence, painted by the artist between 1549 and 1552. The altarpiece of the Resurrection is a tall panel with Christ in the center, rising to heaven. Around Him are various figures, holy, allegorical, and human, among them the reclining figure in this drawing, a soldier who turns to look up at Christ. The entire scene is one of contorted bodies painted in the hard, anatomical style of Bronzino's Mannerism. As many of the figures are nude or have a single swatch of material—the soldier has a scarf across his chest with a serpent's head protruding from the knot at his neck—the painting was severely criticized in the sixteenth century for its licentiousness. Nevertheless, it remains today in the chapel for which it was commissioned.

TITIAN

b. Pieve di Cadore, 1477(?)
d. Venice, 1576

The Rape of Europa

1562
Oil on canvas
178 x 205 cm. (70 x 80 3/4 in.)
Acquired 1896

When a protracted negotiation for Gainsborough's *Blue Boy* collapsed, Berenson was able to offer this, the most important painting in the museum, in its place. Mrs. Gardner immediately snapped it up and thereafter never considered English portraits for her collection.

About 1550, Titian was commissioned by Philip II of Spain to paint a series of *poesie* on mythological subjects. The *Rape of Europa* was first mentioned in Titian's correspondence with Philip's agent in 1559, and in 1562 Titian wrote to say that it was completed and being sent to Madrid. The king's immediate response is not known, but there is evidence of the painting's subsequent influence on the world of art. Rubens made an exact copy which he carried home to Antwerp. Van Dyck kept a sketch of it which now hangs below the picture itself. Both Velázquez and Watteau borrowed passages from it in their work, and Reynolds owned a seventeenth-century copy.

In 1623 the painting was packed up to be shipped to England as a present for James I. Nevertheless, it remained in Spain until it appeared in France in the eighteenth century and then in England early in the nineteenth century. Of the other *poesie,* two are in Madrid, two in Scotland, and two in London. The closest in composition and feeling to the *Europa* is the *Perseus and Andromeda* in the Wallace Collection, London. There is reason to suspect that they were conceived by the artist to be hung in juxtaposition. Indeed all these works could have been assembled as a gallery of *poesie,* not unlike the gallery created by Titian and Bellini for the Duke of Ferrara.

The myth relates how Zeus falls in love with Europa, the beautiful daughter of the Phoenician king. He disguises himself as a white bull and appears to the princess and her handmaidens who decorate his horns with a wreath of flowers. When Europa sits on his back he rushes into the sea and steals her away to Crete.

Titian has chosen this moment to make an operatic setting worthy of the drama. He has left behind the tenets of Renaissance painting and with the surety of genius breaks with common practice to create dramatic effects. The heroine, her face almost covered, is positioned far to the right and appears to be leaving the canvas. The perspective is never entirely clear and seems calculated to project the figures toward us, as though the bull were raised on the crest of a wave. Above and below, cupids gather, anticipating the outcome; one balanced on a monstrous fish seems to mock Europa's plight. Far behind the players in the drama are the figures of the women on the shore and, in the distance, the misty grandeur of a vast mountain range. All of these components are brought together with such control and imagination that we accept the artifice, overpowered by the sheer beauty of color and form that is everywhere evident.

PAOLO VERONESE

b. Verona, 1528
d. Venice, 1588

The Marriage of St. Catherine

Ca. 1575
Ink and gouache on paper
45 x 30 cm. (17 3/4 x 11 3/4 in.)
Acquired 1902

This drawing is remarkably close to the large altarpiece by Veronese for the Church of Santa Caterina, Venice, now in the Accademia. There are significant changes, however, particularly the absence of figures in the drawing: In the painting there are angels in the sky, behind the pair with the music in the foreground and behind St. Catherine. These and other minor changes lead to the conclusion that this is the study for the altarpiece, generally dated 1575. The drawing was finished with great care, unusual in a preparatory sketch, and perhaps was commissioned from the artist after the painting was completed, at which time he simplified his original design.

St. Catherine of Alexandria (third century A.D.) receives a ring from the Christ Child, which, according to her legend, came to her in a dream at the time of her baptism, when Christ took her as his celestial spouse. The ring was on her finger when she awoke, and she wore it the rest of her life. In Renaissance painting she is shown as an adult receiving the ring, or with the emblem of her martyrdom, the spiked wheel, upon which the Emperor Maxentius attempted to kill her.

71

GIOVANNI BATTISTA MORONI

b. Albino, near Bergamo, ca. 1520
d. Bergamo, 1578

A Bearded Man in Black

1576
Oil on canvas
171 x 101 cm. (67 5/16 x 39 3/4 in.)
Acquired 1895

The artist was at his best in portraits, with a deft hand for rendering likeness and sufficient invention to find a dignified, often telling pose. The present nobleman, whose name has not come down to us, commands our attention with his forbidding countenance and confident air. Moroni's composition is simple and the range of color has been limited. Black hair and beard add to the sitter's unwelcoming gaze. The cool background emphasizes the silhouette of his sword and cap, and touches of white at his wrist and neck contrast with a somber attire—all marks of his worldly station. These are the life and breath of the portrait.

Moroni worked in and around Bergamo, accepting a succession of local sitters—some, according to biographers, unwanted commissions sent by Titian. Moretto da Brescia, Moroni's master, was trained by Titian, but little of the warmth or insight of Venetian portraiture can be found in this picture. Moroni's portraits, severe in their treatment but with solidity and presence, seem influenced by Florentine Mannerism, without the extremes that would have been unacceptable in provincial Lombardy.

73

HERRI MET DE BLES

b. Bouvignes or Dinant, ca. 1480 (?)
d. Venice, 1550 (?)

The Story of David and Bathsheba

Ca. 1535
Oil on panel
46.2 x 69.2 cm. (18 3/16 x 27 1/4 in.)
Acquired 1895

Northern European paintings before the seventeenth century are not well represented in the Gardner Museum. The present example provides a glimpse of the world beyond the Alps. The setting and style are Northern, but the costumes are supposed to be Roman or Oriental, in keeping with the tradition for painting religious scenes in classical dress.

Bathsheba, half immersed in the pool to the left, receives the summons from the King's messenger while David, scepter in hand, looks out at her from his balcony at the far right. In a second scene, below, he appears to give her husband, Uriah, a letter to his commander in chief which will place him in the forefront of battle and lead to his death. The elders surrounding them are perhaps perplexed, more likely, disapproving.

The rest of the panel has nothing to do with these events but reflects contemporary court life in its pleasanter outdoor aspects. Women stroll with a dog toward a tennis court, one with a hawk on her arm, and a jester peers through a door at the game in progress. Behind them is a court for another kind of game. In the middle distance are a swimming pool, archery grounds, a maze, and, finally, hunters chasing a stag. We are also treated to the architecture of the palace, a castle, and the surrounding village while ships ply the harbor waters.

So popular was this arrangement that the painting exists in a number of versions, the best of which is at the Hartford Atheneum. That is identified with another artist, but the landscape in it is different, and that which appears in our version identifies the artist as Herri met de Bles (loosely translated as Henry of the White Lock). He is probably the same as Henri de Patinir, who was recorded in the guild of St. Luke in Antwerp in 1535, and the painting may be considered to come from about that period.

HANS HOLBEIN

b. Augsburg, 1497
d. London, 1543

Sir William Butts, M.D.

1543
Oil on panel
46.8 x 37 cm. (18 3/8 x 14 9/16 in.)
Acquired 1899

76

This is the only pair of husband-and-wife portraits by Holbein, who must have painted them in the last year of his life. The artist had been court painter to Henry VIII since 1535 and Butts was the court physician. In 1541, Holbein painted the fresco, *King Henry VIII Grants the Charter to the Barber-Surgeons*, now largely in ruins, in Barbers Hall in the Old City. In it, Butts is on the king's right, behind the principal of the guild, and the present portrait was done from the cartoon for that fresco. The drawing for the portrait of Lady Butts is at Windsor Castle.

HANS HOLBEIN

Lady Butts

1543
Oil on panel
47.2 x 36.9 cm. (18 5/8 x 14 1/2 in.)
Acquired 1899

Although these are pendant portraits, the subjects are treated very differently. Sir William is almost in profile, the face a sympathetic portrait, the costume undistinguished were it not for the fur collar and gold chain. The background was originally an enamel blue, now much worn and darkened, and the inscription is barely visible. Lady Butts has fared much better and is a more ornate work, perhaps, as some critics have said, because the artist was less sympathetic to the sitter and made up for it in this way. At any rate, her costume is enhanced with needlework and jewelry, and her full face framed by an intricate cap. This is Holbein's only portrait of an older woman.

77

PETER PAUL RUBENS

b. Siegen, 1577
d. Antwerp, 1640

Thomas Howard, Earl of Arundel

Ca. 1630
Oil on canvas
122 x 102 cm. (48 x 40 1/8 in.)
Acquired 1898

In 1621, Thomas Howard, Earl of Arundel, became through succession the Earl Marshal of England. We see him here dressed as befits the office and resting on the gold baton. His helmet has blue and white ostrich feathers, further attributes of the Premier Duke of the Realm, a title which rests with the House of Norfolk. On the gold chain is the miniature badge of the Knight of the Garter, which also accounts for his blue sash. A career at court, which he began auspiciously as a favorite to the heir apparent, declined after the latter's death, and he was imprisoned in the Tower of London before being reinstated. After several missions for Charles I, Arundel left England, and had no part in the Civil War except by contribution to the Royalists' cause. He died in Padua in 1646 at the age of sixty-one.

His fame today is secured by his connoisseurship. He was the first great collector of antiquities in England, and possessed a large collection of pictures and a fine library, all of which endeared him to Rubens. In London there are two smaller portraits by Rubens of him. The one in the National Portrait Gallery may be a sketch for the present picture, and there is a drawing of the whole composition at the Clark Art Institute in Williamstown, Massachusetts.

Nothing is known of the commission itself, but in a letter the artist implied that he had seen the Arundel collection. That was in 1629, and the portrait is generally believed to have been done after the artist returned to Antwerp in 1630. It may have remained in his studio at his death, for there are passages on the canvas which seem unfinished. Certainly the head is among the most impressive portraits by Rubens, filled with vitality and aristocratic mien. The sitter's pose recalls the great work of Titian, which Rubens had encountered many times in his travels (and had already paid homage to in his copy of *The Rape of Europa*), and the concept as well as the characterization are equal to that of his best work.

REMBRANDT

b. Leyden, 1606
d. Amsterdam, 1669

Self-Portrait

Ca. 1629
Oil on panel
89.7 x 73.5 cm. (35 3/8 x 29 in.)
Acquired 1896

With the arrival of this painting in Boston early in 1896—the first of four Rembrandts that Mrs. Gardner acquired within a five-year span—she and her husband determined to create their own museum. In later life she referred to it as the cornerstone of her collection because at that moment, as she surveyed what she had and hoped to have, the decision was made. Thereafter, her collecting accelerated and in the end she was able to fill many more rooms than the house on Beacon Street alone contained and to include in the fabric of Fenway Court a number of classical and medieval architectural fragments.

This is one of the very earliest of a long list of self-portraits which record the artist's evolution in style as well as maturity. Rembrandt was living in Leyden in 1629, supposedly sharing quarters with the painter Jan Lievens. The colors, especially the dominant soft hues, are typical of his early manner. The rich variation of tone, from the deep shadow to the highlights of his chain and jewelry, are already marks of his range and competence. The fascination with bizarre costume would return periodically throughout his work, but in the smaller portrait from the same period in the Mauritshuis, in the Hague, he is hatless and dressed in everyday clothing. In both of these portraits, his face meets the viewer with the same penetrating, expectant look.

81

REMBRANDT

A Lady and Gentleman in Black

1633
Oil on canvas
131.6 x 109 cm. (51 3/4 x 43 in.)
Acquired 1898

The husband and wife are placed in the front hall of their comfortable house, and, to judge by their dress, are evidently about to go out. Behind the gentleman there is an oval picture on the wall, either a map or a Chinese painting, and a short flight of steps which leads to the interior.

This is a commissioned portrait from a successful moment in Rembrandt's life, when he was a young but established painter in Amsterdam. The man and his wife, most probably rich burghers, have never been identified. The style is not unlike that used by the better portrait painters of the time, except that in the hands of Rembrandt, portraits always assume an extra dimension. In this case, it is the indefinable tension that the two figures project, she with her meditative gaze into the void, he with his appraising stare directly out of the canvas. The light across the canvas reinforces their contrasting moods and also allows the artist to demonstrate his skill in handling details such as the embroidery on the woman's dress.

The painting did not always look like this. A recent X ray shows an active boy between the couple, his arm raised perhaps with a stick or plaything, or possibly to take his father's hand which now holds a glove. Since we cannot identify the sitters, we do not know why this child was later painted out, but we assume that it was not because he died. The most logical explanation that can be given is that within the confines of this carefully balanced scene, both in mood and composition, the child was a disturbing element. The X ray provokes the further speculation that the chair in the foreground was originally something else, perhaps a sleeping dog. Whatever the reason for these alterations, this is an early example of Rembrandt's mastery of character and his ability to use a familiar setting in an individual way.

83

REMBRANDT

The Storm on the Sea of Galilee

1633
Oil on canvas
161.7 x 129.8 cm. (63 5/8 x 51 1/8 in.)
Acquired 1898

Painted at about the same time as the double portrait that hangs near it in the Dutch Room (page 83), *The Storm on the Sea of Galilee* is as violent as the other is repressed. There are three accounts in the Bible (the most graphic is Luke 8:22–25) of this scene. Christ was asleep in a boat when a great storm struck the craft and the Disciples rushed to him, saying "Master, Master, we perish." In Rembrandt's interpretation, the artist draws from his own memory of storms on the inland waters of Holland for his image of a small sailboat in a tempest. Thus we see part of the company straining to lower the sails, two men speaking with Christ, who disdains their concern, and the others, except for the man at the tiller, in various attitudes of fear, including one who is seasick. The light breaks through the clouds to reveal the white foam, the yellow sails, and the bright costumes in sharp contrast to the dark turbulent water and grey sky. All of these heighten the drama in which only Christ remains calm.

Executed at a moment in which Dutch marine painting was coming into vogue, this is Rembrandt's only known seascape, although he went on to paint numerous large dramatic pictures, often relying on the Bible for his subjects. He would use members of his family or friends as models in these, and several faces in this canvas appear in other works by the artist, but without doubt the man nearest the viewer, looking out of the canvas, is the young artist himself.

REMBRANDT

The Obelisk

1638
Oil on panel
54.5 x 71 cm. (21 1/2 x 28 in.)
Acquired 1900

The forbidding landscape casts its mood over the scene and dwarfs the figures in it. The eye is drawn to the swirling clouds, the battered, fantastic tree in the foreground, the unfathomable depths of the forest, and the succession of natural phenomena that leads back to the horizon. Only upon careful inspection are we made aware of the human scale of the two figures in the foreground, the horse cart on the bridge, the mill, the coach beyond, and the dam at the head of the river near a village. The obelisk stands out in dramatic light, a reminder of the number of such markers that once served as milestones in Rembrandt's Holland. On closer inspection, the man on foot carries a falcon and the rider is accompanied by a dog. But it is the combination of familiar touches with an imaginary landscape that makes the picture remarkable, a document perhaps of man as the insignificant intruder among the forces of nature.

Rembrandt painted only a few landscapes, usually relying on his imagination to interpret nature, while his landscape drawings are apt to be studies from life of the farm buildings and hedgerows near Amsterdam. An obelisk is the subject of an etching done twelve years later, and mountains like the one seen in the distance can be found in his works in other media. Rembrandt was not the first of his countrymen to paint nature as a fantasy, and he no doubt drew on their work while displaying his most subtle use of colors, as though his paint box were limited to a few tones, and the painting were a matter of highlights and earth colors.

87

ANTHONY VAN DYCK

b. Antwerp, 1599
d. London, 1641

A Lady with a Rose

Ca. 1635–40
Oil on canvas
101.5 x 79.5 cm. (39 $^{15}/_{16}$ x 31 $^{1}/_{4}$ in.)
Acquired 1897

The artist was apprenticed as a boy of ten to an artist in his native city, and before he was twenty he was an assistant to Rubens. He went to England in 1620 where he attracted the attention of the court, but soon left to travel and paint in Italy. In a span of twenty years he travelled often and produced a remarkable number of large, well-painted canvases, but he is forever associated with the court of Charles I, where he remained longer than anywhere else and left a record in portraits of the royal family and of English aristocracy from the period before the English Civil War.

Nothing is known of the lady – who is thought to have been English – in this portrait, painted during Van Dyck's longest stay in London, 1635–40. Although it is not among his most forceful presentations, Van Dyck has given the lady a pleasant pose, her arms folded and a rose tucked in the long tapered fingers. It is reminiscent of Rubens's composition, but the style is not his. Van Dyck's success rested on his ability to make his sitters refined and elegant, and unmistakably aristocratic. A delicate coiffure, matched pearls, and an expensive scarf set off the lady's haughty expression, the half smile of ease and amusement. The rose is often associated with England and may have been chosen here as an emblem of love, beauty, or the brevity of both.

88

89

JOHANNES VERMEER

b. Delft, 1632
d. Delft, 1675

The Concert

Ca. 1658–60
Oil on canvas
72.5 x 64.7 cm. (28 1/2 x 25 7/16 in.)
Acquired 1892

The entire picture is controlled by the light pouring in from an unseen window to the left. The artist views his subject almost as though through a lens, defining every nuance of that light, and eliminating all extraneous or peripheral illumination. The domestic scene is the reverse of most contemporary painting in that the viewer is considered least of all. The central figure has his back to us, and the girl at the clavichord has her face in shadow, her back to the light. The scene painted on the lid of the clavichord is obscured by the figures, and the lid's edge lines up too well with the frame of the picture on the left and cuts into the picture on the right. The table is at eye level, so that the instrument on the oriental rug is barely visible, and yet these objects in the foreground stand between viewer and subject. The sheer audacity of the artist in every inch of canvas is a tribute to his genius. Vermeer accomplished in his woefully small oeuvre a singular feat that has remained almost beyond explanation.

His life is only known to us from a very few documents. He was married at twenty-one and had eleven children. Most likely he owned the pictures that appear within his paintings and may have been an art dealer; and he was often in financial difficulty, particularly at the end of his short life. Until the end of the last century he was virtually unrecognized. Fewer than forty works have been attributed to him, and there are no collections of drawings or prints on which to build his biography.

This picture of a concert is typical of the painting for which he is known. In an ordinary room in a Dutch house, three figures are engaged in a concert. Exactly what their relationship is cannot be deciphered. Some critics have attempted to read complex meanings into these simple scenes, and indeed Vermeer did paint two purely allegorical pictures. On the wall are contemporary paintings, that on the right is Van Baburen's *Procuress* (now in the Boston Museum of Fine Arts), the other tentatively identified as Fabritius's *An Inn by the River*. Vermeer's picture demands our attention because we can see so much in this mundane setting. The pattern in the rug or on the chair, the fall of the white skirt, and the reflection off a single pearl have a clarity that only a camera might duplicate. Within this extremity of control the artist has chosen colors and patterns that create a story of their own so that these figures need not have movement or emotion.

The shades of color move from dark into light and back again with ever-changing gradations, and the spaces in the room are thus rendered with such exactitude that we are drawn in, and become an uninvited audience. Like them we are motionless, struck dumb with delight in their silent music.

FRANCISCO DE ZURBARÁN

b. Fuente de Cantos, 1598
d. Madrid, 1664

A Doctor of Law

Ca. 1630–39
Oil on canvas
195.5 x 104.5 cm. (77 x 40 1/4 in.)
Acquired 1910

From his costume, we know this man to be a doctor of law at the University of Salamanca. It is a great tribute to the artist that this painting can hold its own in the brilliant company of the Dutch Room at Fenway Court, and in fact it was, in 1867, sold as a portrait by Zurbarán's great contemporary, Velázquez. The influence of the latter is evident in the grandeur of the pose and in the way the hand falls on the chair. A comparison may be made with Velázquez's portrait of Philip IV of about 1630, also in the museum. A date for the picture of the doctor has never been determined exactly, but there is every reason to believe it to come from the 1630s, after the artist had taken up residence in Seville. The sitter has never been identified even tentatively, but it would seem to be among the earliest of Zurbarán's lay portraits. Much of his work was for the Church, and portraits of members of religious orders or persons idealized as saints were far more common. Here, the face is modelled with a smoothness that conveys little of the character behind it, yet the rich colors of the green curtain and darker green hat, the scarlet hood, and the warm tone of the wall lend an interest and presence to this academic. The only breaks within these fields of color are the nails and leather on the chair and the linings of his gloves; in his right hand he holds the left one, just removed, which gives a touch of immediacy to an otherwise formal presentation.

93

GIOVANNI BATTISTA TIEPOLO

b. Venice, 1696
d. Madrid, 1770

The Wedding of Barbarossa

1749–50
Oil on canvas
71 x 55 cm. (28 x 21⁵⁄₈ in.)
Acquired 1900

In 1749, Tiepolo was invited to come to Würzburg by Prince-Bishop Karl Philipp von Greiffenklau, in order to decorate the Kaisersaal of the Residenz. He received the dimensions of the room and a program for the three themes drawn up by a court historian. The subjects were to be events from the life of the Holy Roman Emperor Frederick Barbarossa (1150–90): *The Wedding of Barbarossa to Beatrice of Burgundy*, which took place in Würzburg in 1156; *Barbarossa's Investiture of Bishop Harold von Hochheim with the Duchy of Franconia*; and *Apollo Bringing Beatrice to Barbarossa*. The artist arrived in the city from Venice in December 1750 with his sons, Domenico, then twenty-three, and Lorenzo, fourteen, and remained there until November 1753 in order to complete a second contract, the frescoes over the great staircase leading to the Kaisersaal.

Prior to leaving Venice, Tiepolo had prepared the present sketch. Painted to demonstrate to his patron what his fresco would look like, this scene has all the majesty of a royal wedding, and yet the artist, within this splendid setting, includes a small dog on the steps in the foreground—a caprice not used in the fresco. In the fresco, a more horizontal format was integrated into the cove at the end of the ceiling, which is concave in both directions. By framing the scene with painted and gilded curtains held back by *putti* modelled completely in the round, a more or less triangular opening was created for the scene. The steps were lengthened to the right, the perspective was made deeper, with the figures behind the railing at the top seen through the arch which replaced the wall with the niche figure in the oil sketch. In the fresco, the Prince-Bishop's features, drawn in profile, are used for the face of the officiating bishop, and Barbarossa has been placed between the bride and the bishop so that he may face the viewer. At the other end of the large room is the fresco of the investiture of Prince Harold, a sketch for which is in the Metropolitan Museum of Art, New York, and the third scene, of Apollo bringing Beatrice to Barbarossa, is painted across the ceiling.

The London National Gallery has another version of the *Wedding*, of about the same size, but with some of the changes mentioned above, including the portrait of the Prince-Bishop. It is generally regarded as a work by Domenico Tiepolo, executed at Würzburg.

EDOUARD MANET

b. Paris, 1832
d. Paris, 1883

Madame Auguste Manet

Ca. 1863
Oil on canvas
98 x 80 cm. (38 1/2 x 31 1/2 in.)
Acquired 1910

96

Mrs. Gardner was always fond of good portraits, and as a group they hold an important position in the collection beginning with the early fifteenth century and continuing to portraits by her contemporaries. This portrait shows Madame Manet dressed in widow's black and was probably painted soon after her son was married and she came to live with them. The expression and pose are severe, and the limited palette hardly modifies the somber effect. The dark background pushes her blacker dress to the front of the canvas, and her small figure, at almost life-size, seems to fill the space, defined on the right by the red chair cover. Her striking appearance is marked by piercing blue eyes set in the pallid flesh of old age, contrasted with the warmer shades of her brown hair and gold jewelry. She is a study in opposites: frail, determined, challenging, withdrawn, alert, relaxed, and the personification of dignity.

EDGAR DEGAS

b. Paris, 1834
d. Paris, 1917

Madame Gaujelin

1867
Oil on canvas
61.2 x 45.7 cm. (24 1/8 x 18 in.)
Acquired 1904

Degas's sitter was a ballerina who had commissioned the portrait and rejected it, complaining that it did not do her justice. She sits on a white divan beside her white dressing table. Her dress is flecked with spangles. The crimson on either side of her may be the lining of her coat, which emphasizes her slim figure. This portrait has many similarities with that of Madame Manet (opposite), who is shown on a black background and is also wearing black. Madame Gaujelin's pensive mood is in sharp contrast to the lively background; her head is set off by the angular fields of color behind her, and it is modelled in a richer palette than the ivory tones that describe Madame Manet's face and hands. Here the space, the furniture, the colors are never exactly defined, but in this, as in the other portrait, the depth of her calm expression holds our attention.

EDGAR DEGAS

Leaving the Paddock

Undated
Pencil and watercolor on paper
10 x 16 cm. (4 $1/8$ x 6 $3/8$ in.)
Acquired 1919

At the sales from Degas's studio in 1919, Mrs. Gardner was able to get, through her agent in Paris, four of the eleven items which she instructed him to buy. Another drawing, a study of a ballerina, was purchased the following year.

Many of the artist's drawings were made to capture a certain pose or detail, often repeated several times on the sheet as, for example, the two drawings of a jockey which were acquired with the present sketch. In addition to the jockeys, Mrs. Gardner also bought a drawing of a racehorse and *Cortège aux Environs de Florence*, perhaps a study for a large canvas, now in the Louvre, entitled *Semiramis Building a City*. The racetrack fascinated Degas for a time early in his career, but by 1882 he seems to have gone on to other subjects, notably the ballet.

What is particularly engaging about the present sheet is that it is more than a study sketch, and may have been planned for a larger scheme. Although the right side is only roughly blocked in, the rest is nicely finished, including the sky. The horse and jockey in the center received the greatest attention. The left side of the drawing, with a group of men in front of a building, is an interesting touch of informality. The colors are fresh and enliven the sense of a crowd and the spirit of a sporting scene of the kind that Degas also presented in small oil paintings.

JAMES ABBOTT McNEILL WHISTLER

b. Lowell, Massachusetts, 1834
d. London, 1903

Harmony in Blue and Silver: Trouville

1865
Oil on canvas
50 x 76 cm. (19 3/4 x 30 in.)
Acquired 1892

In 1879, Mrs. Gardner attended the exhibition of paintings at the Grosvenor Gallery, London, where she saw Whistler's portrait of Connie Gilchrist. Not long after, she went with Henry Adams to a party given for artists by Lady Lindsay, owner of the gallery, and there she met Whistler. During the 1880s she visited his studio and acquired a small painting and a pastel. He did a portrait of Mrs. Gardner in pastel at that time. This canvas was bought in 1892 from his studio in Paris, where she returned in 1895 for another painting and a pastel. There is a cabinet of Whistler's etchings in the museum, and in a case of works on paper by Whistler and Sargent are several of his drawings, a packet of his letters, his photograph, and his thin bamboo cane.

Sargent and Whistler, both expatriate Americans, were trained in Paris, but beyond that they had little in common. Throughout his life Whistler accepted controversy and prided himself on his aesthetics, which he expounded in writing and exemplified in his daily life. Although many canvases appear simple, he often labored over his work, toying with an idea for more than a decade, and became diverted by schemes that involved new ideas for paintings, room designs, or combinations of both. Even his titles were calculated to evoke another dimension, such as his *Harmonies* and *Nocturnes*.

With Courbet he painted seascapes in Trouville in the summer of 1865. In the present picture, Courbet is standing on the beach and, except for distant sails, is the only intrusion in this flat, untroubled panorama. Whistler's modulated colors capture the subtle gradations of sand and sea under a bright summer sky. The harmony of shades devoid of shapes or suggestion of movement, conveys a sense of a vast world seen through a filter, an aesthetic closer to our own age than to the Victorian world decried by the artist.

JAMES ABBOTT McNEILL WHISTLER

The Little Note in Yellow and Gold

1886
Pastel
27 x 14 cm. (10 5/8 x 5 1/2 in.)
Acquired 1886

This was the first portrait of Mrs. Gardner and was followed by Sargent's in 1888, Bunker's in 1889, Passini's in 1892, and Zorn's in 1894. Sargent and Zorn also made drawings of her. *The Little Note in Yellow and Gold*, charming though it is, tells us less than the larger portraits, but conveys, as all do, a sense of Mrs. Gardner's vitality. Another pastel, bought from the artist in 1895, is of a nude reclining on a couch, lying on her side facing the viewer. In this small scale, the face is not unlike that in the portrait. Mrs. Gardner, with good humor—anticipating what people would say—hung the two beside each other.

In a letter to Mrs. Gardner, Whistler wrote, "Of course to paint the little picture will be a joy." He later asked a friend to call on Mrs. Gardner in Paris and to mention that he got five to six hundred guineas for a large full-length portrait and might do a little picture for one to two hundred. He concluded the letter with: "Then I might ask about 150." Mrs. Gardner paid a hundred guineas.

THOMAS WILMER DEWING

b. Boston, 1851
d. New York City, 1938

A Lady in Yellow

1888
Oil on panel
50 x 40 cm. (19 3/4 x 15 3/4 in.)
Acquired 1888

Mrs. Gardner acquired certain objects in the collection on the recommendation of friends, a number of them artists whose own work she had admired and bought. Dewing's study of a woman in a yellow dress is a typical example. It was bought through the help of the Boston painter Dennis Bunker, a young friend encouraged by Mrs. Gardner. Bunker may have known Dewing at the time; they certainly met later, when Bunker went to live in New York.

To Mrs. Gardner, who was travelling in Spain in April 1888, Bunker wrote: "I have to assure you that the Dewing picture is yours. It is now on exhibition [Boston Art Club] and is having a perfectly tremendous success as it deserves. . . ."

The style is not unlike Bunker's own style, that of the Boston School of painters; the sitter seems lost in meditation and is placed in front of an obscured background. Much care has been given to the material and to the details of the chair, and the flesh tones have the quality of fine porcelain. Dewing began his career in Boston before studying in Paris from 1876–79. He returned to Boston and thereafter lived in New York. Charles Freer admired his work and acquired twenty-seven paintings, eleven pastels, and three silverpoints, which were hung together in a room in the Freer Gallery in Washington when it was opened to the public in 1923.

105

JOHN SINGER SARGENT

b. Florence, 1856
d. London, 1925

El Jaleo

1882
Oil on canvas
237 x 352 cm. (93 1/4 x 138 5/8 in.)
Acquired 1914

El Jaleo is the name of a Spanish song and dance, and Sargent most likely conceived the idea for this picture while watching the flamenco in Andalusia during the winter of 1879–80. At that time, the influence of Spanish culture pervaded Paris, where Sargent was a pupil in the studio of Carolus-Duran. In Spain, he copied Velázquez in the Prado and sketched in the streets and cafes. The painting was begun on his return to Paris, where he employed Marie Renard, a professional model, to pose for the dancer. At the same time he did another painting of the Spanish dance (Hispanic Society of America, New York). Throughout his life Sargent was fond of Spanish music. He kept flamenco records in his studio in Boston, and gave a set to Mrs. Gardner. At about the same time, he gave her a book of sketches associated with this painting.

This painting was Sargent's most successful youthful work and perhaps his greatest subject painting. It was finished in time to be exhibited in the Paris Salon of 1882, where it received acclaim. One critic commented that it "reveals the most remarkable qualities of observation and intention." His powers of observation had been forged since youth on his travels through Europe, which he recorded in numerous sketch books. His intention was to capture the momentary intensity of what he had witnessed, the straining of the dancer, the fervor of the guitarists and rhythmic clapping by the chorus. In the end it is far grander theater than the humble stages of the flamenco, and more music hall than night club. The shallow stage is lit from below; the swirling costume at *eye* level, the dancer's raised arm caught in a stylized movement. Behind her black mantilla, a head is thrown back in song. Two guitars on the wall over the vacant chair define the narrow space. In each figure as in the whole assembly, the feeling of the moment is apparent.

So great was its success that the painting was immediately bought by a New York art dealer, from whom a cousin of Jack Gardner's, T. Jefferson Coolidge of Boston, acquired it in 1887. He gave it to Mrs. Gardner when she constructed the Spanish Cloister in 1914, where it hangs opposite the entrance to the museum.

107

JOHN SINGER SARGENT

Isabella Stewart Gardner

1887–88
Oil on canvas
190 x 81.2 cm. (74 3/4 x 32 in.)
Acquired in 1888

Mrs. Gardner met Sargent in 1886 in his studio in London, where she was introduced by Henry James. His portrait of Madame Gautreau, known as *Madame X*, had been the scandal of the Paris Salon of 1884, both because of the sitter's reputation and the gown, which revealed a great deal. Naturally Mrs. Gardner was anxious to see it and naturally she wanted her portrait painted by the charming American who had grown up in Florence.

Sargent arrived in Newport in 1887 and after completing several commissions there he proceeded to Boston, where he began work in the Gardners' house at 152 Beacon Street. Mrs. Gardner related that she refused the first eight versions. Sargent believed she was trying to dismiss him, but she insisted he make a ninth try, nine being a mystical number and therefore significant to her. The result was accepted and pronounced by her the finest work he had ever done.

The portrait has been likened to an icon because of its stiff, frontal pose and halo-like background. An elaborate design, borrowed from a piece of material that remains in the collection, covers the background and surrounds her head like that of a deity. The stark pose and the prominently placed jewelry call attention to her figure—a figure well thought of in those days when a woman's arm was regarded as a thing of beauty. Her face was distinguished by eyes set far apart, but not by her mouth, which was terribly plain and has been played down by the artist.

The painting was exhibited at the St. Botolph Club in Boston at Sargent's first American exhibition. Mr. Gardner overheard a remark about it at his club (having to do with the décolletage) and had it removed from the exhibition, refusing to permit it to be put on public display in his lifetime. When the museum was built it was placed in the Gothic Room, and during Mrs. Gardner's lifetime the room was closed to the public.

109

JOHN SINGER SARGENT

A Tent in the Rockies

1916
Watercolor on paper
39.2 x 53.2 cm. (15 $^7/_{16}$ x 21 in.)
Acquired 1916 (?)

Encouraged by friends, Sargent determined that he must see the Canadian Rockies, and set off in the summer of 1916 with his batman to camp and paint in the vicinity of Lake Louise, British Columbia. All was not serene, as he wrote Mrs. Gardner, as the rain put a damper on his otherwise exuberant nature. He managed to paint two canvases, *Yoho Falls*, now in this museum, and *Lake O'Hara* in the Fogg Museum, Harvard University. However, this watercolor of his tent was a masterpiece of the kind that he most enjoyed, the sketch of a simple scene caught without special arrangement but with the true sensitivity of an artist who understood the effects of color.

The tent in which the two slept, with its white canvas and birch poles, is wonderfully presented in shades of white, while the towering pine forest has a different texture and forms a shadowy backdrop to the sunlit tent. The camper's provisions are barely suggested in the interior.

Several other drawings and watercolors from this adventure survive. The medium was congenial to Sargent's gentlemanly nature and he seldom sold his sketches, preferring to give them as presents or keep them on his own walls. His watercolors in general represent his enthusiasms for nature and architecture and often for the pleasure he found in their details. The museum has about a dozen such works, many of Venice. Mrs. Gardner bought a number of them at auction, for which Sargent scolded her for paying the exorbitant prices. This one he gave her directly.

110

JOHN SINGER SARGENT

Mrs. Gardner in White

1922
Watercolor on paper
42.3 x 32 cm. (16 3/4 x 12 1/2 in.)
Acquired 1922

This picture is inscribed *To my friend Mrs. Gardner/John S. Sargent*. Mrs. Gardner wrote Berenson, "Did I tell you of Sargent's wonderful sketch in water-colour of me which keeps every one's tongue busy wagging? Even I think it is exquisite. As it was utterly unpremeditated both by him and by me, I think that is its main reason for being so good."

The idea was evidently Sargent's, as he wrote from the Copley Plaza Hotel in Boston in September 1922, "It is very nice of you to be willing to let me try a water-colour . . ." and it must have come at a time when Mrs. Gardner, used to being at the center of things, was almost a recluse. The stroke she suffered at the end of 1918 meant that she could barely get around, although occasionally she went out in a car.

Only family and a few friends were allowed to call as she sought to conceal the severity of her illness. Sargent, of course, was always welcome, and the painting of her portrait again after thirty-five years of friendship no doubt pleased both of them.

He had long given up the full-scale portraits in oil for which he is now best remembered. His work was almost entirely restricted to watercolors done for himself, charcoal portraits as commissions, and major decorative commissions such as the murals for the Boston Public Library and the ceiling decorations for the Boston Museum of Fine Arts. These last consumed most of the final years of his life.

Mrs. Gardner was eighty-two at the time and would live less than two years more. The portrait shows her determination and lucidity, traits which stayed with her to the end of her life.

112

113

ANDERS ZORN

b. Dalecarlia, Sweden, 1860
d. Dalecarlia, Sweden, 1920

Mrs. Gardner in Venice

1894
Oil on canvas
91 x 66 cm. (35 3/4 x 26 in.)
Acquired 1895

Mrs. Gardner met Zorn at the Chicago Columbian Exposition of 1893 in front of his painting *The Omnibus* which she purchased. A lifelong friendship was thus begun and Zorn came to Boston early in 1894 to make a portrait of her. This was an etching which did not please her and she asked that the artist sell her the entire edition. Commissions from other patrons in Boston done in oils were more successful and a pastel of her remains in the Blue Room, a gift of the artist.

In October the Zorns visited the Gardners at the Palazzo Barbaro in Venice, and the artist caught this chance pose of Mrs. Gardner in the doorway to a balcony, lit from the fireworks on the Grand Canal in the background. It is an interesting contrast to the Sargent painting (page 109), in that both artists were trained in the same tradition and painted in similar styles. The true comparison here is not with Sargent's portraits, which have the quality of posed photographs, but with his figure paintings (*El Jaleo,* on page 107, for example) which capture an instantaneous movement or expression in broad brushstrokes and sharp contrasts. In addition to a large collection of Zorn's etchings—for which he is justly famous—Mrs. Gardner acquired several other canvases, along with *The Omnibus*, the study for his portrait of Mrs. Grover Cleveland, a portrait of A. Piat Andrew, and one of a mother and child bathing in a lake in Zorn's native Sweden, where he most often worked.

115

HENRI MATISSE

b. Le Cateau-Cambrésis, 1869
d. Cimiez, 1954

The Terrace, St.-Tropez

1904
Oil on canvas
72 x 58 cm. (28 1/2 x 22 3/4 in.)
Acquired 1912

This fine example of an early work by one of the great artists of the twentieth century came as a present to Mrs. Gardner around 1912, and was thereby the first Matisse to enter an American museum. The artist was visiting Paul Signac on the Riviera when this canvas was painted. He experimented for a while in the Pointillist style for which his host is known, but neither that technique nor the vibrant colors which identified him with the Fauves a year later are dominant in this painting. The style, one that was highly decorative in its use of simple broken patterns played against broad bands of color, would appear again off and on during the next twenty years. His wife's kimono as she leans against the boathouse is the focus for the painting, but our pleasure is in the overall effect of shimmering daylight on contrasting surfaces. In all of his great works he exhibited a color sensitivity that makes his paintings inimitable, and, in spite of the apparent ease with which he seemed to accomplish this, was often occupied for weeks on one canvas.

Among the friends who early recognized his genius, many of whom were English or American, was the archeologist Thomas Whittemore. He presented this picture with five drawings by the artist to her.

117

LEON BAKST

b. St. Petersburg, 1866
d. Paris, 1924

Costume for Ida Rubinstein

1911
Pencil and watercolor on paper
28 x 21 cm. (11 x 8 1/4 in.)
Acquired 1913

Bakst's name is forever associated with the Ballet Russe under the management of Serge Diaghilev, but his work and his career were much broader. He began work as an illustrator, and soon was teaching and painting portraits. Diaghilev, whom he had met in 1890, published a magazine between 1898 and 1902, and after 1899, was editor of *The Annual of the Imperial Theater*. Bakst contributed portraits and decorative drawings to these and soon was designing for theater and ballet in Russia. He continued to work in Russia until 1912 and with Diaghilev in Paris until 1916 but his frequent commissions for other impresarios annoyed his old friend and they parted with some bitterness. He continued to design for the theater up to the moment of his death and realized a certain fame through exhibitions of his paintings and designs in Paris, London, and the United States.

When the Ballet Russe arrived in Paris in 1909, Bakst's designs caused a sensation. The sets were a complexity of oriental motifs, one

LEON BAKST

Costume for Anna Pavlova

1913
Pencil and watercolor on paper
31 x 24 cm. (12 1/4 x 9 1/2 in.)
Acquired 1913

laid upon another, the colors explosive, even to an audience that had experienced the paintings of the Fauves, and the costumes, drawing on folk art, were interpreted with artistic abandon. The combination was dramatically successful and soon inspired imitators in the theater, in fashion, and in interior design.

Neither of these drawings were for Diaghilev productions. The Martyrdom of St. Sebastian, with Bakst's sets and costumes, was produced at the Chalet Theater in 1911 with Ida Rubinstein in the title role. The book was by D'Annunzio, the music by Debussy, the choreography by Fokine. In 1913 the Oriental Ballet, with music by Seroff, Moussorgsky, and Rimsky-Korsakov and choreography by Zaglich was produced in the Royal Opera House, London. One of the costumes for Pavlova was probably this; a second drawing with a similar inscription is in the Boston Museum of Fine Arts. Mrs. Gardner acquired both of the drawings seen here in the same year that a touring exhibition of Bakst's designs came to Boston.

The Titian Room

This gallery, its walls covered with a rich crimson damask, is named for Titian's *Rape of Europa*, perhaps the best known painting in the collection. The work of another Venetian artist, Vincenzo Catena, is placed above the door leading to the Long Gallery and a portrait of Philip IV of Spain by Velázquez hangs to the right.

Sculpture and Decorative Arts

ROMAN

Archaistic Torso
of a Goddess (?)

Late Republican, ca. 50 B.C.
Pentelic marble
76.2 cm. high (30 in.)

The figure's dress is an Ionian chiton, a loose garment that hangs in deep folds and is buttoned at the sleeves. Another garment is thrown over the shoulders and falls down her back. The head, now missing, was perhaps that of the goddess Artemis (Diana of Roman mythology). It was made separately, and the neck inserted behind the string of large beads that would have covered the line where the two pieces joined. One leg is slightly advanced to modify the frontal pose, reminiscent of the caryatids on the Acropolis.

Small bronzes from the Archaic and Archaistic periods in Greek art provide examples of the complete figure, with its typical drapery, from which this sculpture was derived. In marble, it may be compared with the Artemis found at Pompeii or the torso in the Museo Archeologico, Florence, from the first century B.C. A further comparison with the Orestes and Electra in Naples suggests that it may have come from the atelier of Pasiteles, circa 50 B.C.

123

GRAECO-ROMAN

Peplophoros

First century A.D. Roman copy of a
　　Greek original of ca. 455–50 B.C.
Greek marble
Dimensions without plinth: 148 x 78
　　x 48 cm. (58 1/4 x 30 3/4 x 19 in.)
Plinth: 8.5 cm. high (3 3/8 in.)
Acquired 1901

The peplos, or loose outer garment cut in a rectangle, is rendered here as a heavy woolen Doric chiton. The lower part was pulled up through a belt covered by the fold at the waist. The upper edge falls from a clasp at the shoulder, and is represented as sewn along the right side from the waist to the hem. From the back, the left arm appears to have been extended in the act of adjusting the material, which is caught up on that side. The figure stands on her left foot; the right knee is bent and breaks the folds of the peplos.

The figure may have been a goddess, a youthful Persephone, or a mortal, as both were presented in sculpture dressed in this fashion. Deep carving of this kind suggests that the marble could have been a copy of an earlier bronze. A bronze *Dancer* in Naples, found at Herculaneum, is another case in which Greek sculpture of the middle of the fifth century influenced later Roman work.

The statue came from the Gardens of Sallust in Rome, the general area where the marble *Odysseus*, also in the collection, was found at an earlier date. An export license was not granted until 1936, although Mrs. Gardner had arranged that it would eventually be placed where it now stands in the central court of the museum.

GRAECO-ROMAN

Torso

Julio-Claudian, first century B.C.–first
    century A.D.
Large-grained Greek island marble
47.5 cm. high (18 3/4 in.)

From the remaining portion of the neck, it is evident that the head was turned to the subject's left. Part of the support for the figure can still be seen on the left hip, and the left arm may have extended out to rest on top of it. His weight was on his right leg, and the right arm was held away from the body. The full form of the trunk, with muscles not entirely revealed, is typical of the fourth century B.C., and indeed, parts of a replica were found in the Athenian Agora. The original may have been a Hermes or was perhaps closer in type to the Niobid sculptures, now in the Uffizi, Florence. Another torso in the Prado, Madrid, similar to this, is dated in the Julio-Claudian period, The lovely, large-grained marble is from the island of Thasos at the northern end of the Aegean.

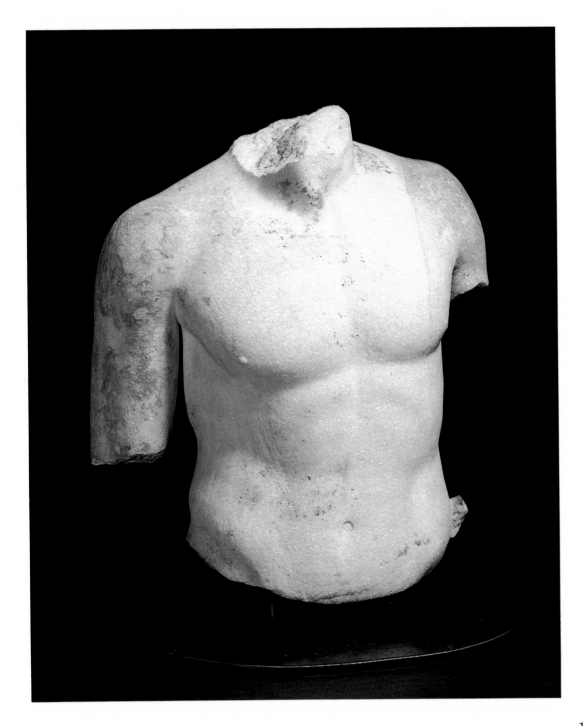

GRAECO-ROMAN

Torso of Dionysos

Antonine, 140–190 A.D.
Coarse-grained Greek (?) marble
92 cm. high (36 1/4 in.)

The figure was supported by a vine stump behind the left leg, and fragments of the stem of the vine and of grapes and leaves remain at the side. On the right shoulder are traces of a fillet from a wreath. His weight was on his right leg, as he bent forward, with the left arm raised, presumably to pluck grapes, as in some other existing versions. Two curling locks of his long hair fall on his shoulder. The turn of the shoulder and the raised hip emphasize the sensuality of the figure and convey a sense of indolence. These traits all identify the figure as a Dionysos.

This popular pose goes back to the resting satyr (or marble faun), perhaps to the Hermes by Praxiteles (ca. 300 B.C.). Examples may be seen in the museums of the Rhode Island School of Design and Princeton University.

129

GRAECO-ROMAN

Relief of a Maenad or Hora

First or second century A.D.
Pentelic marble (?)
143.5 x 58.5 cm. (56 1/2 x 23 in.)
Acquired 1897

Seven marble panels with dancing maidens were found in Rome in 1908 which, with the present example, formed the decorative base for a circular altar or funerary monument. Somehow this one had been separated from the group, uncovered at an earlier date, and reduced in size for display by itself. Its history prior to 1897 is speculation. In its original place, the upraised right arm would have extended onto the adjoining marble, where part of the scarf may still be seen. Details were lost when the edge was cut back on the present figure, but all of the other figures have a raised frieze, a vine with buds, leaves, and flowers, along the top. The maidens are dancing on their toes and the movement of the group was carefully calculated to be read from any point in the circle, some maidens moving to the right, others to the left, in a complicated pattern. The costumes, faces, and hairstyles vary from panel to panel.

The prototype for this figure came from the latter part of the fifth century B.C., and a relief of a dancing maiden in the National Museum in Athens with the same hairstyle is an indication of the source. The other seven panels of this group are joined together in the Museo delle Terme, Rome.

131

ROMAN

Mosaic Pavement

Second century A.D.
500.5 x 495.5 cm. (197 x 195 in.)
Acquired 1897

Excavations begun in 1863 in Montebello, eight miles north of Rome, uncovered a house that had belonged to Livia Drusilla, widow of Octavius Caesar and mother of Claudius, both Emperors of Rome. This imperial villa and its lands occupied the entire hill. A smaller residence was uncovered in 1892, perhaps a small bathing establishment, to judge from the heating system. In it were seven mosaics, three in good condition. One was bought at the end of the century by an American and then given to the Metropolitan Museum in New York. A second was bought by Mr. and Mrs. Gardner in 1897, for what was to be the Gardner Museum.

The pattern, as with all mosaics, is made from small colored tesserae, in this case, stones (whereas in medieval wall decoration stones with a glass surface are used). The basic pattern is in black and white, but red, yellow, green, and grey were used as accents. In the center is the head of Medusa, with wings and snakes instead of hair. This is surrounded by a ribbon design, and the rest of the center is filled with linking flowered scrolls with a different bird in the center of each side. The border is a double guilloche in white on black and beyond that a design of scrolls inside a narrow black line.

The Metropolitan Museum's mosaic, found in the room next to that with the Gardner mosaic, has in the center a scene with two figures not yet identified. A third mosaic from the building, present location unknown, had a small figure of Bacchus in the center and a floral pattern of bindweed, with birds, winged *genii*, and kraters at the corners. The building was erected in the reign of Hadrian (117–38 A.D.) and the floors were presumably laid at the same time.

ROMAN

Sarcophagus with Satyrs and Maenads Gathering Grapes

Severan, 222–35 A.D.
Pentelic marble
105.5 x 224 x 101.5 cm. (41 1/2 x 88 1/8 x 40 in.)
Acquired 1898

Bacchanalian subjects were used on Roman sarcophagi up to and into the fourth century. Scenes of gay abandon, seemingly at odds with the utilitarian purpose of the tomb, were a forecast of the desired afterlife of the deceased. This large and elaborately carved marble has attracted attention since it first appeared in an inventory of the sixteenth century, then passing through several famous collections before it was sold to Mrs. Gardner.

The arrangement and workmanship across the front and the two ends show great artistic perception. The twelve main figures shown here are satyrs and maenads, alternating and paired, yet each group connected with the next. The corner figures are posed like herms supporting the rim, which is composed of an arbor of grapevines. A second group of *putti* are tucked beneath the feet of the larger figures. Silenus as a herm is on the left end and Ariadne reclines on the right end. Dionysos is missing, unless he is the youth carried by a second Silenus on the back side. A panther, associated with Dionysos, figures in the carving on the front and again on the back, where an eagle and swan are also included among the satyrs and maenads.

The carving and finish of the back of the sarcophagus are very different, being in low relief and left with the tool marks unpolished. The frieze along the front was never completed on the back. The feeling of the group there is also different, less organized, and it has been suggested that it was never finished because it would have been against a wall.

The stone lid for such a sarcophagus would have had a life-size reclining figure representing the deceased. The revelling figures were inspired by Hellenistic painting, and also appear on a sarcophagus in the Museo Capitolino, Rome.

SPANISH

Christ from a Deposition Group

Second half of the twelfth century
Polychromed wood
122 cm. high (48 in.)
Acquired 1917

The crucified Christ was the central figure of a group with Nicodemus and Joseph of Arimathea. The scene was thus a *tableau vivant* illustrating one of the moments of Christ's Passion. Two such groups of the Deposition survive in Spain; in both of these one of Christ's arms remains attached to the cross, with Nicodemus in the act of removing it, while the other arm and the weight of Christ's body are supported by Joseph of Arimathea. From a comparison with these it was possible to establish the place of origin of this figure in Catalonia.

From the eleventh century onward, Lenten and Easter Liturgy became significantly more important in the church year, with a concomitant production of religious objects to illustrate the scenes of the Passion. Many were made of wood, which was covered with gesso and painted. Traces of original color may be seen on all parts of the present example, and holes indicate that there was once a crown.

When, in 1916, this figure was found in New York, the right arm had been straightened to make it a figure on a crucifix, and hair, a crown of thorns, a beard, and a linen dress had been added. When the restoration was completed and the figure was revealed as it had been intended, it was praised for the unusually fine carving, both in the lines of the body and for the quality of the face and head, conveying Christ's triumph over death.

SOISSONS

Stained Glass Window

First half of thirteenth century
366 x 157.5 cm. (144 x 62 in.)
Acquired 1906

Many of the mysteries surrounding the origin and meaning of the stained glass window over the altar in the museum's chapel were revealed in an article published in 1960. (L. Grodecki, "Les Vitraux Soissonais du Louvre, du Musée Marmottan et collections américaines," *La Revue des arts*). The author has found various panels—once in the Cathedral at Soissons—in the Louvre, the Musée Marmottan, the Corcoran Gallery, the Gardner Museum, and formerly in Berlin (now lost). Of interest to us are the comparisons between the present window and that in the Louvre, both of which contain scenes from the same legend and may once have been part of a single large window.

The legend is that of the martyrdom of Saints Nicaise, Archbishop of Rheims, and his sister Eutropie, who defended the cathedral against invasion by the Vandals in the fifth century. Both saints were beheaded, after which St. Nicaise arose and placed his head on the altar. A celestial army arrived to drive off the Vandals. Since the windows were smashed at some point in history, the story was rearranged and recreated between the present windows, with additions to fill out the design. In our window, the lower register has the beheading of Eutropie, and Nicaise placing his head on the altar. The second register shows the mourning over Eutropie and a garbled scene with an excellent surviving panel, perhaps intended to be the people of Rheims listening to Nicaise. The two windows in the next register are devoted to the burial of Nicaise, while angels above carry the souls to heaven and other angels, at the very top, hold the martyrs' crowns. The other scenes in the story, the arrival of the Vandals, the death of Nicaise, and the rout of the Vandals, occupy the Louvre window. In some instances, particularly the upper registers in the present window, the restorers may have copied older scenes, but the effect of a fine thirteenth-century window comes through to the viewer, calling to mind the great age of cathedral building. These are examples from an important period in the development of Gothic art, and may be dated between 1205 and 1230.

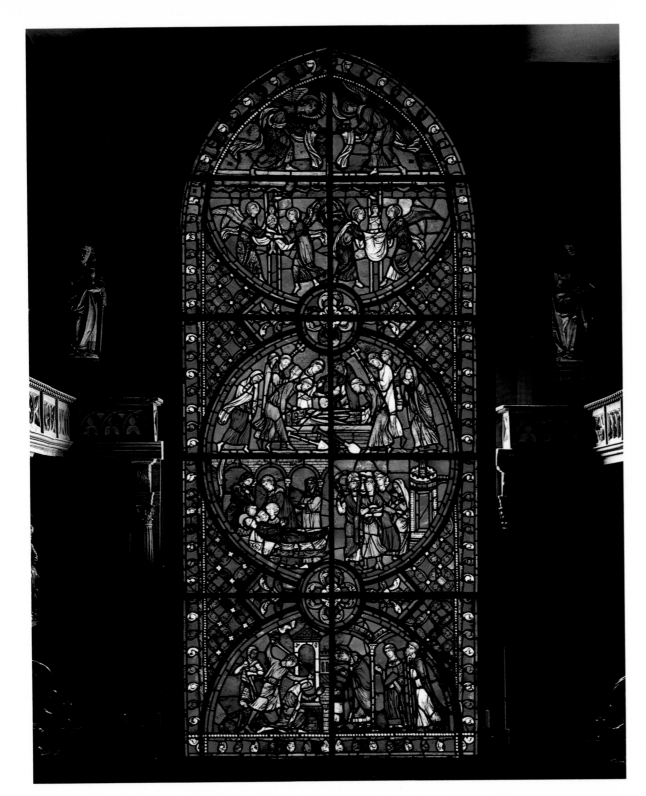

SIENESE

Angel of the Annunciation

Late fourteenth century
Polychromed and gilt poplar
167.5 cm. high (66 in.)
Acquired 1899

This life-size figure of the angel Gabriel, and its companion piece, probably the Virgin in the Musée Jacquemart-André, Paris, were made for a church in Tuscany during the fourteenth century. Although the attribution is not secure, they have been published as youthful works of the Sienese sculptor Domenico di Nicolo dei Cori (1363–1453). Within the church, the pair might have been placed on either side of the main altar or possibly on the transept wall on either side of the entrance to the choir. They fit into the fourteenth-century tradition of wood sculptures of the Annunciation, of which there are still a number to be seen in the churches in and around Siena.

Gabriel's upraised hand indicates that he is delivering his message. The Virgin is posed with her left hand on her heart and her right extended in a gesture of surprise. The pair was still together in 1898 at a dealer's in Florence, where the Virgin was the first to be sold, and where Mrs. Gardner discovered the angel the next year.

141

FLORENTINE

Chasuble with Scenes from the Life of Christ

Early fifteenth century
Brocatelle and embroidery
121 x 73.5 cm. (47 1/2 x 29 in.)

142

The decoration of this chasuble, scenes from the life of Christ, was originally made for the edge of a cope, a floor-length cape worn by the clergy in processions. Two of the scenes were cut diagonally to fit at either end of the cross that traditionally appears on the back of a chasuble, worn by the celebrant for a church service. Between the fragments are panels with Saints John the Evangelist, Paul, and Peter.

Below are the Adoration of the Magi, Christ disputing in the Temple, and Christ in the House of Levi. The panels on the front have the following scenes: the Annunciation, Nativity, Circumcision, Baptism, and Resurrection. The scenes would have been arranged chronologically along the front edges of the cope and the saints would have joined the edges behind the wearer's neck.

143

LORRAINE

Retable with Scenes of the Passion

Ca. 1425
Limestone
78.5 x 274.5 x 21.5 cm.
  (31 x 108 x 8 1/2 in.)
Acquired 1899

The eight Gothic arches of this retable, or altar shelf, present six scenes of the Passion with the two outside arches occupied by the donors, kneeling in prayer, and their patron saints. Reading from left to right, the scenes are the Arrest, showing the Kiss of Judas, the Flagellation, Christ carrying the Cross, the Crucifixion (which includes the arch beyond with the mocking figures), the Descent from the Cross, and the Three Marys at the Tomb, with the Roman soldiers asleep in front of it. The partitions, with capitals and bases, are surmounted with pinnacles, and in the spandrels above, half-length figures of the prophets with scrolls occupy smaller windows.

This retable's place of origin was established by the existence of a similar work in Vignory (Haute-Marne) in the Church of St. Etienne. Both retables have the same donors, and derive from an atelier of sculptors active in Lorraine and Champagne at the end of the fourteenth century and through the first three decades of the fifteenth. The exact location of this shop is not yet known but there is reason to believe that it was located in Joinville, its style influenced by sculpture in the neighborhood of Cologne and the Middle Rhine. The style is marked by a pleasing composition and attention to detail rather than powerful figures and individual expression.

The donors, Guillaume Bouvenot, whose coat of arms is at his feet, and his wife, Gudelette, are buried in the chapel of St. Barbara where their names appear in an epitaph. Both retables are thought to have been commissioned at the same time, and on this assumption are dated during Bouvenot's lifetime, ca. 1425. As the chapel was founded by a *bailli* of Saint-Dizier and Vignory, who died in 1340, it is logical that the donor occupied a similar position and sought to have this retable as a second monument to his family, perhaps for another church such as Saint-Dizier.

144

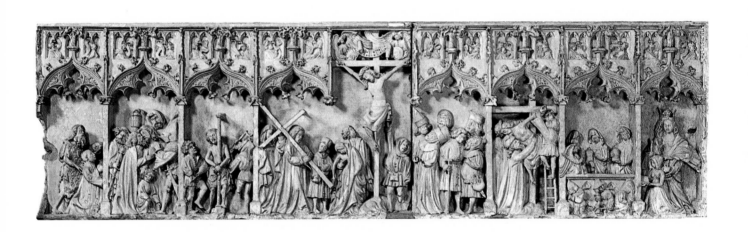

FLEMISH, TOURNAI OR ARRAS

The Fulfillment of the Curse on Ahab

1460–70
Tapestry: wool warp, wool and
  silk wefts
373.5 x 452.5 cm. (147 x 178 in.)
Acquired 1897

The final scenes in the story of the curse of Ahab, as told in the Old Testament, are here presented much like a modern cartoon sequence, with the hero, Jehu, appearing in each scene. The viewer was expected to know that Ahab, who succeeded his father as King of Israel in about 875 B.C., provoked bitter opposition among orthodox Jews because he "went and served Baal and worshipped him." His queen, Jezebel, was accused of stealing vineyards near the palace by arranging for the owner's death. The prophet Elijah laid God's curse on Ahab and his family. Ahab, through contrition, had the curse postponed to his sons' reign.

In the tapestry, Jehu, leader of the revolt, is seen by a watchman in the tower (top, center) approaching the city of Jezreel with his army. Ahab's son is killed by Jehu's arrow (bottom, left) and slumps in his chariot (behind the man on horseback who turns to see what has happened). The scene above may be the army of Jehu chasing Ahaziah, King of Judah, who was visiting the court at the time of the revolt.

In the center of the tapestry, Jehu, with crown and scepter, enters through the gate of the city and commands the eunuchs in the window to throw down Jezebel. Jehu then wrote letters to the rulers of Jezreel, and to the elders, saying that those who would be loyal followers should "take the heads" of Ahab's sons. One of the letters is being delivered in the tower to the right. The command was obeyed and the heads delivered to Jehu, who is seen inspecting two of them in a chest in the final scene (bottom, right). Thus, the curse of Elijah was carried out.

The tapestry has been cut on all four sides. By comparison with one of two tapestries of the story of Jephtha in the Cathedral of Saragossa, possibly from the same workshop, as much as forty-three inches may have been lost in the vertical dimension. The right side appears to be intact (except for the original border) but the left has incomplete figures. The inscriptions, in Picard dialect, are quotations from the Bible. These were moved; the one on the right was originally on the left, the others farther to the right.

In all probability, the Ahab tapestry was one of a series, either devoted to this story or each tapestry depicting a passage from the Old Testament. They would have hung together in a large, late-medieval hall, so that the guests could enjoy the decorative qualities of the tapestry from every angle: the individual scene from nearby, or the overall effect from afar.

FLORENTINE

The Divine Comedy

Landino Commentary, illustrations
  from designs by Botticelli
1481
Page: 41 x 27.5 cm. (16 x 10 3/4 in.)
Illustration: 9.5 x 17.8 cm. (3 3/4 x
  7 in.)
Acquired 1887

Mrs. Gardner's introduction to Dante came from the novelist F. Marion Crawford, who had grown up in Italy and was fluent in Italian. Together, during the winter of 1881–82 they read *The Divine Comedy*, and shortly thereafter, Mrs. Gardner joined the Dante Circle that met in the house of Professor Charles Elliot Norton. He encouraged her to begin a collection of rare books and manuscripts.

In addition to this, the first Florentine edition of the poem, the collection includes the Brescia edition of 1487, the Aldine portable edition of 1502, and a fourteenth-century manuscript.

Cristoforo Landino, a leading Neoplatonist and member of the Medici household, supplied the commentary (standard for over sixty years) and Lorenzo di Pierfrancesco de'Medici sponsored the printing and publishing. As the latter was Botticelli's most faithful patron, the artist was enlisted to make the drawings for the plates.

The book was designed to have a plate with each canto, yet only those for the *Inferno* were printed, perhaps because Botticelli was called to Rome to work on the Sistine Chapel, or because of the cost and difficulty. Whatever the reason, only the first two or three plates were printed on the pages; the others were printed separately and pasted in. Our edition has three printed pages of illustrations, with the second repeated before the third canto. Over it has been pasted the third illustration, with numbers four through nineteen pasted in their proper places.

These were made from copper plates, quite possibly the work of Baccio Baldini, a goldsmith, whose interpretation of Botticelli's drawings lacks the depth and beauty of the original sheets. This copy is one of the few to have all nineteen illustrations. The binding by Francis Bedford is brown crushed levant morocco with gilt decoration.

Illustrated here is the plate before the second canto. The opening in the hill is the gate to Hell and above it is printed PER ME, the first words of the third canto. (This inscription was repeated on the third illustration also.) Dante and Virgil appear twice—once on the left, where Dante hesitates to follow Virgil, and then on the way to the hill, where Virgil reassures him by showing him the vision of Beatrice.

tiene dell'httmana generatione et laltre chose fanza la cognitione et fede delle quali fecondo la christiana re
ligione neffuno puo andare alla beatitudine Et nondixe non cognofci ma dixe non conofcefti che non cono
fcefti in uita ma alprefente conofci. Et forfe e/ da dubitare fe lanima laquale mentre fu congiunta col corpo
non hebbe cognitione di dio. Dipoi feperata gia et dannata lapoffa hauere: Nientedimeno fice nclude dathe
ologi che lanima feperata dal corpo ha tanto acume che non per congetture lequali poffono effere falfe: Ma
per ragioni dimoftratiue conofcono la luce et bellezza di dio effere infinita laquale cognitione da loro graffi
fima pena uederidofi di quella effer priuati; Ma non la conofcano diftinctamente perche di tale cognitione
piglierebbono fommo gaudio et participerebbono del fommo bene. Chome uerbi gratia Se uno giouinet
to non fuffi ftato infirenze al tempo dellannuale celebratione et pompa facta al Baptifta et uno gli narraffi
quella effere molto bella in modo che altuffo et fanza dubitatione el giouinetto cupidiffimo di tali fpectacu
li lo credeffi non e/ dubbio che ne piglierebbe difpiacere non piccolo uedendofene priuato; perche intende
la bellezza in confufo che non fa altro che accendergli la uoglia dintenderla diftinctamente et con fuo ordine
ACCIO ch'io fugga quefto male; cioe el male della ignorantia et del uitio. ET PEGGIO; cioe ladannatione
laquale feguita dal non conofcere quanto male fia nel uitio. Chi non conofce quanto fia peftifero eluitio nõ
lo fugge di che confeguita graue detrimento; et diquefto ne nafce unaltro piu graue perche non lo fuggen
do ne fa habito elquale uccide lanima. SI CH'IO ueggia la porta di fan Pietro; Per quefto intendi lentrata
del purgatorio. Impeche Pietro cioe elfommo potefice et tutti efacerdoti equali hãno lauctorita da quello ab
foluédo lanima dalla colpa lafanno habile apotere andare apurgarfi: et non effendo abfoluta farebbe dannata
allinferno. Ne'mi pare che fi debbe intendere laporta del paradifo perche Virgilio difopra ha dimoftro nõ
effere fufficiente a condurlo. ALLHOR fi moffe: Danthe che e/lappetito rationale et la ragione inferiore
priega la ragion fuperiore che lo guidi alla contemplatione et allhora la ragione excitata dallap petito fi uol
ge alla contemplatione et Danthe cioe epfo appetito gli tien dricto perche gli euenta obbediente

CANTO SECONDO DELLA PRIMA CANTICA

I

O giorno fenandaua et laer bruno
togleua glianimali che fono interra
dalle fatiche loro: et io folo uno
Mapparecchiauo a foftener laguerra
fi del camino et fi della pietate:
che ritrarra la mente che non erra
O mufe o alto ingegno hor maiutate .
o mente che fcriuefti cio ch'io uidi
qui fi parra la tua nobilitate.

P

Offiamo dire che elprecedente capitolo fia ftato
quafi una propofitione di tutta lopera p laquale
lauctore non folamente dimoftra con brieue pa
role quello che p tutta lopera habbia adire; Ma ancho
ra la ragione perche tiene tale ordine. Deftoffi lappeti
to ricercãdo el fuo bene et illuminato dalla ragione fug
gi la felua: et faliua al monte doue uedea el fole. Ma p
lauia delle fiere; dalle quali gli fu uietato el falire. Ilche
fignifica che conofciuto ma non molto diftinctamente
chel fommo bene confiftua in fruire idio: cercaua la co
gnitione di quello nella uita ciuile doue regna la ragio
ne inferiore: Laquale fpeffo e/ingannata dal fenfo : Et
doue effendo leuirtu ciuili non perfecte molto poffono

le perturbationi dellanimo lequali cercando piacere honore et utile non feguitano eluero gaudio Ne ancho
ra el uero utile che non fi puo mai feperare da lhonefto. Ne el uero honore elquale non e/ altro che la uera

SIENESE

Cassone

Sixteenth century
Gilt and gesso on wood
59.7 x 167 x 54.6 cm. (23 1/2 x 65 3/4
   x 21 1/2 in.)
Acquired 1894

Chests are among the few kinds of furniture known to have existed in the Middle Ages. They served as a seat, a low table, or a portable trunk. During the Renaissance, artists were employed to decorate these chests, which became much more sophisticated objects. The marriage chest, or *cassone*, one assumes, came to the bride with necessities for beginning her new life. A number of examples are in the museum; often, however, only the front panel was saved to be displayed as a work of art, such as the pair of chest fronts with triumphs painted on them by Pesellino.

The present marriage chest has been gilded all over except for the back. Across the front are twelve women and seven men at a wedding. They are in low relief and portrayed in a frieze-like arrangement against a pattern of oak leaves tooled into the gold. There is a raised decorative border. Flesh tones are used on the faces of the wedding party and for the winged heralds dressed in Roman armor with dark paint for hair, their features, and on the coats of arms to right and left. A dark green paint was used for the floor under the figures.

The coat of arms, which is part of the decoration on the lid and either end of the chest, is that of the Sienese family Piccolomini. On the left it has been quartered with that of the Todeschini. Pope Pius II was a Piccolomini and his nephew Pius III was the son of his sister, who married a Todeschini. On stylistic grounds the chest must be dated later in the century than their marriage, and was probably made during or soon after the papacy of Pius II when Pius III was still archbishop of Siena. It was probably intended for the wedding of one of his nephews.

151

MINO DA FIESOLE

b. Florence, 1429
d. Florence, 1484

Relief of a Woman

Ca. 1475–80
Carrara marble
33.5 x 28 x 10.5 cm.
   (13 1/4 x 11 x 4 1/8 in.)
Acquired 1899

This charming profile of a woman, often thought to be a portrait, came from the Palazzo Antinori (now Aldobrandini) in Florence. A copy now in the Palazzo was presumably made when the original was sold at the end of the last century. Another similar relief of a woman, but in Renaissance dress, is in the Museo Nazionale, Florence, with the inscription ET IO DA MINO OAVVTO ELLVME (and I by Mino have seen the light). Despite the similarities, the museum's relief is closer to several works by Mino of classical derivation, notably in the profile "portraits" of *A Roman Emperor* in the Boston Museum of Fine Arts, the *Caesar Aurelius* in Florence, and the *Scipio* in Philadelphia.

These marble reliefs have the flat, irregular folds consistent with all of Mino's work. There is a marked similarity in the strong, carefully modelled features and the artist's individual attention to a complicated hair style. In each case the frame is cut into the marble and the bust fills the space, often spilling over the frame at top and lower sides. In the present instance, the braided hair seems to be modelled on a work of classical sculpture which Mino could have seen in Florence or during his periods of work in Rome.

153

MATTEO CIVITALI

b. Lucca, 1436
d. Lucca, 1501

The Virgin Adoring the Child

Ca. 1480
Polychromed and gilt terracotta
99 x 103 x 38 cm. (39 x 40 1/2 x 15 in.)
Acquired 1902

In all of Tuscany Matteo was the only major fifteenth-century sculptor in marble working outside Florence. Most of his work is still in his native town of Lucca. He is known to have worked in terracotta, and, among the pieces attributed to him, the group in the Gardner Museum has the greatest claim to being from his hand. There is every indication that his training was in Florence, but on his own he developed a distinctive style, and often a surprising diversity in his treatment of subjects.

The present example of his work displays not only a serene beauty in the Virgin at prayer, but the unusual concept of the Virgin teaching the Child to pray (or possibly reciprocal adoration), which is found in paintings of the period but not in sculpture. The ease and grace with which he has dealt with a large terracotta is evident in the treatment of the Virgin's cloak, which is pulled in around her knees and falls over her feet on one side and under the Christ Child on the other. The large folds are nicely contrasted with the delicacy of her features, the strands of her hair falling over her dress in front, and the gilt decoration on the neck and sleeve of the garment. Her gaze and the attitude of the figure concentrate her devotions on the plump, lifelike child, who bends toward her to complete the composition.

155

GIOVANNI MINELLI

b. Padua, ca. 1460
d. Padua, ca. 1527

The Entombment of Christ with the Figure of Carlotta Lusignan

Ca. 1483–87
Polychromed terracotta (wooden
frame added in the nineteenth
century)
91.5 x 114.5 x 12.5 cm. (36 x 45 x 5 in.)
Acquired 1897

This presentation of the Entombment with the dead Christ supported by the Virgin and St. John has a particularly poignant history, centered on the figure of the child who appears with the group. She is Carlotta, an illegitimate daughter of James II, the last king of Cyprus from the house of Lusignan. The Cypriot throne was established in the name of the French family following the fourth Crusade, when a number of kingdoms, principalities, and duchies were established for knights of the crusade. The last king married Caterina Cornaro in order to establish an alliance with Venice. Because of the turmoil in and around Cyprus, the royal family was removed by the Venetians following James's death. A report in Venice that the King of Naples wished to kidnap Carlotta and marry her to his son Alphonso, caused the Venetians to carry her to Padua, and there she died in 1480 at the age of twelve.

The altarpiece, donated in her memory by her grandmother, was placed in a chapel in the Paduan church of Sant'Agostino in 1483 and consecrated in 1487. Her grave was at the bottom of the steps to the altar. In 1829 the church was demolished and the terracottas removed to a private chapel, from which the owners sold them to a dealer in 1897.

The figures are all modelled in three-quarter relief and have been repainted, but are otherwise in good condition. They were bought as the work of the older Paduan sculptor Bartolommeo Bellano, whose influence was particularly strong in Minelli's work at this point. The documents identifying the sculptor and the history of this group were published in 1907.

The group is a worthy memorial to the young princess, whose beautiful effigy is suitably pious. The frame was bought in Florence at the same time as Mrs. Gardner acquired the sculpture, but has no relation to it.

156

157

BENEDETTO DA MAIANO

b. Florence, 1442
d. Florence, 1497

The Madonna and Child

Ca. 1494–97
Polychromed and gilt terracotta
104 cm. in diameter with frame
     (41 in.)
Acquired 1899

Benedetto, active in Florence for a period of some thirty years, was slightly younger than the generation of marble carvers around Antonio Rossellino, for whom he most probably worked as a young man, and older than the generation of Michelangelo and the High Renaissance. He was thus the inheritor of a strong tradition, which he carried on with competence, and often with excellence, particularly in his portrait busts. More than any fifteenth-century sculptor, he is known for his terracotta models, a number of which were left in his studio at the time of his death.

This *Madonna and Child* is a variation on a marble tondo by Benedetto for an altarpiece in a chapel in the church of Sant'Agostino at San Gimignano, near Siena. The design is an extension of two earlier works by Rossellino, in the churches of San Miniato, Florence, and Monteoliveto, Naples, the latter commission finished by Benedetto before 1490. The Christ Child in Rossellino's San Miniato tondo and that in Sant'Agostino are seated; a standing Child was used by Benedetto with a Madonna in the roundel now in Santa Maria della Misericordia, Florence, and which was in his possession at the time of his death. Comparison with this late commission suggests that the Gardner tondo was a work of his last years.

The frame, which may have been done after his death, is based on still another work, his tondo for the Strozzi Tomb. Additions made to the sculpture to fill the frame, notably beneath the cushion, are further evidence that it was not necessarily presented as a tondo by the artist. A coat of white paint was applied to suggest marble. The composition has the sweetness and invention of his best works; it is a good example of the Florentine Renaissance delight in the youthful Madonna and her idealized Child, which in painting found its parallel in Botticelli's work, such as *The Madonna of the Eucharist* in this collection (page 47).

159

GIOVANNI DELLA ROBBIA

b. Florence, 1469
d. Florence, 1529

Lamentation over the Dead Christ

After 1514
Glazed polychromed terracotta
250 x 160 cm. (98 3/8 x 63 in.)
Acquired 1899

The second and most famous of the sons of Andrea della Robbia, Giovanni worked in his father's shop, which during his father's long life expanded considerably. His uncle Luca and his father developed distinctive styles, but that of Giovanni is sometimes confused with his brothers' and other members of the workshop whose names are known. For that reason it is difficult to attribute a work to his hand, even though the commission and payment may be recorded in his name.

Behind the Magdalen, an angel is speaking to the three Marys at the Tomb. The hill of Calvary with the three crosses is on the opposite side. Two angels support Veronica's handkerchief in front of the Cross, with the crown of thorns around it. A sun and a moon in the arch refer to the biblical statement that both appeared in the sky at the moment of resurrection.

The frame is made up of multicolored flowers, a motif associated with the Della Robbia shop in the sixteenth century and imitated thereafter by makers of ceramics in and outside of Florence. The inscription reads: O VOS OMNES QVI TRANSITIS PER VIAM ATENDTE ET VIDETE SI EST DOLOR SIMILIS SICVT DOLOR MEVS (Oh all ye that pass by, behold and see if there be any sorrow like unto my sorrow).

Among the works accepted as by Giovanni is the large altarpiece in the Museo Nazionale, Florence, dated 1514–15, very similar in design to the present piece. While the former is larger, with space on either side of the main group and a better landscape, the body of Christ is perhaps more impressive here than in the Florentine arrangement, where his head is supported by both the Virgin and St. John. As noted by one critic, the melodramatic effect is heightened in the Gardner altarpiece, but the proportions are less pleasing. The supposition is that this altarpiece followed the other in time, probably within the same decade.

161

FLEMISH

Proverbs

1475–1500
Tapestry: wool warp, wool and
    silk wefts
282 x 221 cm. (111 x 87 in.)
Acquired 1905

This hanging was woven as a series of unrelated figures or pairs of figures on a field of flowers which rises steeply to the horizon line and a distant mountainous landscape. Nine proverbs are depicted, now severely contained but originally with more field and a border, now missing. The proverbs have been interpreted as follows (left to right): the man who spends his wealth before he gets it is shown eating his wheat before harvest time; the man who holds two candles to the devil countenances wrongdoing and is here handing the second candle to the demon on the column (also interpreted as hypocrisy); the man who prepares to "bell the cat" is about to perform a heroic deed or begin a difficult task; the next man "blows hot and cold" and is shown carrying a bucket of water and a firebrand; the man in the middle clearly "falls between two stools" and can't make up his mind; the next man in sumptuous costume who bites the pillar is the hypocritical churchgoer.

Below, a woman slips a blue hooded cloak on a man; the implication is that she has made him the cuckold. The woman beside her reaches for the purse of the man about to embrace her because she marries him for his money; the last scene cannot be deciphered, but someone holds something to the chin of the old man.

The tapestry is Flemish in style and the fact that seven of the proverbs exist both in French and Flemish texts of the period has led to the supposition that the tapestry was made in a center of weaving on the border between Flanders and France, Tournai or Arras. A number of these proverbs are found in English as well, and probably other languages. A complete literary source may one day be found for the more common English phrases by which we identify them.

162

163

UPPER RHENISH
OR SWABIAN

St. Elizabeth of Hungary

Ca. 1490
Lindenwood
119.5 cm. high (47 in.)
Acquired 1893

The saint's tender face is framed by a nun's wimple, and her figure wrapped from head to toe in flowing garments carved in long, angular folds. The left knee is bent, suggesting movement, and the line of the mantle has been drawn up across the left arm. The sadness and simplicity inherent in her features are set off by the liveliness of the drapery. Delicate fingers hold a loaf of bread and once held a pitcher of wine, the symbols of her charity as well as of the Eucharist.

Herself a queen, Elizabeth is the patron saint of queens. She was born in 1207 and her husband was Louis II of Thuringia, Germany. Widowed at a young age, she was evicted from the castle by her brother-in-law and joined the order of St. Francis of Marburg. Four years after her early death in 1231, she was canonized in honor of her tireless work among the sick and poor. Her magnificent shrine is in Marburg in the church that bears her name. The present sculpture must have originated near that city, where an active cult continued to worship her long after her death.

165

BAVARIAN OR TYROLEAN

St. George

Ca. 1500–10
Polychromed and gilt wood
149 cm. high (58 1/2 in.)
Acquired 1897

The young saint rests one foot on the dragon, holding it for the fatal thrust of his lance. The relatively small beast emphasizes the stature of the saint, carved life-size and to be seen from below by the congregation in a church. Yet, the effect is one of delicacy, in the way he handles his weapon, in the long slim body, and in the shimmering pattern of his armor.

Although the artist has not been identified, the figure was purchased in Munich and has the characteristics of South German wood sculpture. St. George was depicted from the late Middle Ages through the Renaissance, and his legend provided artists with the chance to show the chivalrous knight saving the beautiful damosel. According to that popular legend, a dragon infesting the countryside was offered a princess as sacrifice. George pinned the dragon with his lance and then slew him with his sword, the scene depicted in the painting by Crivelli on page 37.

167

NORTH GERMAN, LÜBECK

Altar of the Trinity with St. Catherine and a Bishop Saint

Ca. 1510–20
Oak
152.5 x 128.5 cm. (60 x 50 1/2 in.)
Acquired 1897

Christ and God the Father are placed between St. Catherine and a Bishop, possibly St. Nicholas. The enclosure is modern; the only remaining part from the original altarpiece is the tracery across the top. At one time, wings, painted or with sculptured figures, would have extended out on either side. At Catherine's feet is a diminutive figure of the Emperor Maxentius, her tormentor, and she holds a spike from the wheel on which he attempted to execute her. The depiction of God seated with Christ on the "throne of mercy" dates from at least the twelfth century. In this instance Christ is presented displaying his wounds from the Cross, and the crown on God's head, a rounded triangle, represents the Trinity.

The sculptor of this group worked with Bernt Notke in northern Germany, Denmark, and Sweden. An altarpiece at Hald, markedly similar in style and perhaps by the same hand, has the unusual inscription *Imperialissima Virgo Maria* below the carved figure of the Virgin, and the sculptor is referred to as the Imperialissima Master. Another work connected with him is in the Copenhagen Museum.

169

SAXON

Altar of the Holy Kinship

Ca. 1510–20
Polychromed and gilt lindenwood
Central panel: 155 x 105.5 cm. (61 x
    41 ½ in.)
Wings: 155 x 52 cm. (61 x 20 ½ in.)
Acquired 1897

This intricate altarpiece is devoted to the relatives of Christ, over whom, at the very top, God the Father presides. Christ, in the very center, receives a bunch of grapes from St. Anne and an apple from the Virgin Mary. Maria Salome and Maria Cleophas are seated on either side with their children. Six male parents are arranged on a balcony, and like the women are dressed in contemporary costume. The saints on the wings are depicted in their traditional garb with their attributes: Catherine with a sword, Margaret with a cross (now missing), Barbara with a castle, and Dorothea with her basket of roses and the child who received it. Four male saints are painted on the outer sides of the wings: Pope Urban I, St. Martin, St. George, and St. Roch.

The story of the Holy Kinship came from the Golden Legend, written by Jacobus de Voragine in the thirteenth century as a compilation of all the stories surrounding the saints, the Virgin, and Christ. It had a great influence on Christian iconography. In the present example, the three Marias were daughters of St. Anne by three different husbands, an attempt to reconcile conflicting statements by the Evangelists, and to unite Jesus with both Jameses, John the Evangelist, Joseph the Just, Simon, and Jude. The Holy Kinship in art was popular in Northern Europe in the fifteenth century, and more or less disappeared after the Council of Trent.

BAVARIAN

St. Martin and the Beggar

Ca. 1520
Polychromed lindenwood
124.5 cm. high (49 in.)
Acquired 1897

The group is in high relief, made to be placed against a wall, which accounts for the saint's quarter turn, a technique used on a number of reliefs of the period. As with our St. George (page 167), the figure's gaze is directed to the congregation and not to the deed at hand, and the proportions of the figures are unrealistic so that the saint may receive the preponderance of detail. He is dressed as a nobleman and wears the typical costume of his age, a doublet with slashed collar and sleeves over short breeches. The crippled beggar dressed in rags carries a pouch and dagger belted around his waist—touches familiar to the contemporary viewer. He reaches up to grasp the cloak that Martin with his sword (now missing) is cutting in half.

The saint, born in Hungary circa 315 A.D., was forced by his father to join the army and while serving in France one winter performed the act of charity for which he is remembered. That night he saw Christ in a vision that caused him to leave the army and to found a monastery. Against his wishes he was made Bishop of Tours and may be depicted in Bishop's habit as well as in military attire when not represented as he is here.

172

173

FRENCH

Chest

Ca. 1540–50
Oak
85 x 164 x 66 cm. (33 1/2 x 64 1/2 x
   26 in.)
Acquired 1897

Considering the large amount of decorative carving on it, this chest has survived in excellent condition, although it may at one time have been gilded and painted. The carving combines the more advanced Italian style with French Gothic elements. Among the latter are the linenfold decoration on the side panels and the half-length figures on the balconies above the niches. The wood is oak, often used in Northern European countries. On the wrought iron lock are the *fleurs-de-lis* of France under the image of the Madonna and Child and separating two profile portraits in roundels.

The saints have their names printed in gothic letters along the bottom. St. Claude is blessing a nun, perhaps a pilgrim; St. John's cup has a serpent, signifying poison, falling from it, put there by Emperor Domitian; St. Barbara holds her attribute, the tower where she was confined; St. Nicholas is in the act of resurrecting three murdered children. The Madonna and Child follow the Northern tradition but an Italian influence may be seen in the poses of the saints, in the pilasters between the niches, and in the *putti* holding up the curtains.

FLEMISH, WORKSHOP OF JAN DER MOYEN

Queen Tomyris Learns that Her Son Spargapises Has Been Taken Captive by Cyrus

1535–50
Tapestry: wool and silk
427 x 468 cm. (14 x 15.4 ft.)
Acquired 1905–06

The story of Cyrus the Great, founder of the Persian Empire, appealed to the tapestry weavers of the sixteenth century. There is a set of five scenes from his life in the Gardner Museum, one of which we see here, and another, different set with ten scenes in the Royal Collection, Madrid. Versions of both series may be found in collections here and abroad. The life of Cyrus the Great as told by Herodotus presented the designers with the opportunity to illustrate political intrigue, courtly settings, battles, and predestined events in a mixture of classical history and legend familiar to the age. The figures appear in contemporary costumes and the landscape and architecture is that of Flanders.

The five scenes are as follows: first, King Astyages, King of the Medes, realizing the future threat to his throne of his infant grandson, Cyrus, decrees that the child be abandoned in the wilderness. Second, Cyrus, now a man, receives the message from Harpagos that the Medes are ready to revolt and join his Persian army in the overthrow of the King. Third, Astyages hands Harpagos the sword, symbol of command of the army. Fourth, Tomyris, Queen of the Massagetai, receives a proposal from Cyrus, which she will refuse; this leads to the scene shown in this tapestry, in which a messenger informs her that her son has been captured in the battle against Cyrus.

The Queen is on the right, walking in a garden with three attendants behind her; two others are conversing in the foreground. There is a battle raging in the background, the second encounter between Cyrus and the Queen's son, in which Cyrus was victorious. The three figures in the middle distance have been interpreted as soldiers returning from celebrating the victory of the first battle. In the rolling landscape are two cottages with thatched roofs.

Flanders in the sixteenth century was the center for some of the finest tapestry weaving of any period, the moment when designers and weavers collaborated to produce works comparable to fine murals. The colors blend harmoniously, surrounded by rich borders. The figures move against an arcadian landscape with gestures and expressions that convey the story.

The weaver's mark on this and one other of the series identifies him as Jan der Moyen who, no doubt, was responsible for all five. He was an important tapestry weaver in Brussels. The tapestries were in the Barberini collection in Rome before coming to this country.

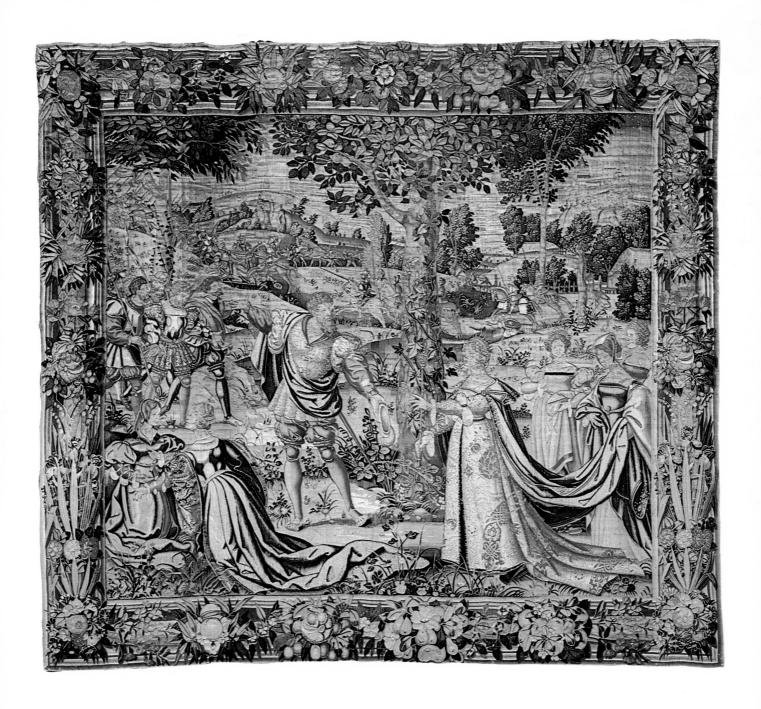

177

BENVENUTO CELLINI

b. Florence, 1500
d. Florence, 1571

Bust of Bindo Altoviti

Ca. 1550
Bronze
105.5 cm. high (41 1/2 in.)
Acquired 1898

Certainly among the first rank in any list of Mrs. Gardner's collection is the bronze bust of Bindo Altoviti by that vainglorious sculptor Benvenuto Cellini. His autobiography has made him better known to a broad public than his surviving work, which may be seen in only a few cities of the world. The bust of Altoviti is one of only two portraits still extant, and his work as a goldsmith is known only through the ornate saltcellar commissioned for Francis I of France, now in the Kunsthistorisches Museum in Vienna. Yet he was among the earliest and most successful Italian artists in disseminating the art of the Italian Renaissance north of the Alps.

Apprenticed at an early age to his father, Cellini ran away from home at the age of fourteen and presented himself in Pisa as a goldsmith, such was his precociousness. For almost twenty years he worked under the patronage of the papal court in Rome, until an unfortunate murder made his departure necessary. He returned from France to his native city of Florence in 1545. At that time he was commissioned by Altoviti; his willingness to serve him and at the same time his known enemy, the duke of Florence, Cosimo, whose marble bust he completed in 1547, tells us something about Cellini's independent nature. The present portrait was completed before his most famous work, the bronze *Perseus*, which was placed in the Piazza della Signoria in 1554.

In his autobiography, he described making the *Perseus* in detail but alludes only tangentially to the Altoviti commission, which was a financial disaster for the sculptor. Altoviti was of a banking family. His father had moved from Florence to Rome, and there Bindo's success may be measured by the number of artists he patronized: Jacopo Sansovino, Raphael, Benedetto da Rovezzano, Vasari, and Francesco Salviati. Through his friendship with Michelangelo, who gave him one of the cartoons for the Sistine ceiling, Bindo was responsible for a letter of praise Cellini received from the older sculptor for this portrait bust.

As a young man, Bindo sat for Raphael and that portrait is now in the Washington National Gallery. He also appears on a medal in which he looks much as he does here. The fall of drapery across the front of the bust, and the general form of the piece suggest a classical figure, but the extraordinary skill with which the beard is presented, the vertical lines of the shirt beneath the jerkin, and the contemporary hat (a net with a device worked in the front) afford it a realism that is reinforced by the aging features. The rampant wolf on the base is from the sitter's coat of arms.

179

ENGLISH OR FRENCH

A Man and Woman in a Garden

Ca. 1590–1610
Needlepoint embroidered hanging: linen
   embroidered with wool and silk
193 x 279.5 cm. (76 x 110 in.)
Acquired 1893

This is a large and beautiful example of needlework of a style that was carried on in several countries, and perhaps by persons of one country working in another. The exact attribution is therefore difficult, but England and France are indicated by the costumes and comparison with similar pieces.

There are a few examples of needleworked furnishing fabrics of this period that were copied after prints showing scenes from history or mythology in contemporary costume. In this case there is no known literary or artistic source. The panel's purpose was purely visual and not utilitarian, as it was meant to be hung on a wall, unlike one placed on a piece of furniture.

The lady and gentleman in this needleworked hanging are walking in a garden, perhaps the park of a large estate, populated with a remarkable collection of animals and birds, including dogs, deer, sheep, rabbits, squirrels, monkeys, owls, a lion, a lizard, and a unicorn. Except for a bagpiper on the left, it might be the Garden of Eden. From the costumes of the couple, the hanging may be dated around 1600. Such clothing was fashionable at the court of Elizabeth I and James I in England, or Henry IV in France. Indeed the work could have been done by aristocratic ladies and their maids, if not by professional embroiderers.

The border has as much detail as the central scene and includes a single fruit tree with animals in each of four rectangular compartments top and bottom. The sides have a rose tree over geese on a pond on one, and daisies, jonquils, and carnations above geese on a pond over a peacock on the other. Allegorical figures in fashionable costumes sit in the corner, with different attributes for each: a lance and shield, a peacock, a pruning knife and sheaves of wheat, and a vase of flowers.

181

ITALIAN

*Garment Fabric for
Ceremonial Occasions* (detail)

1500–1750(?)
Silk, pile-on-pile velvet
119.3 x 63.4 cm. (47 x 25 in.)

This material now in the form of a chasuble, is of a very particular design which had its place in the history of Venice. It may be seen in two works of art in the collection: the portrait of Zacharias Vendramin from Tintoretto's studio, and the anonymous marble bust of a Venetian Senator. In both cases, the men wear this material as a stole, and from numerous other examples, including the costumes in the Museo Correr, Venice, we know that this was the official material for Senators and Procurators in Venice for more than 250 years. It is possible that doges and other officials of the Venetian Republic wore the fabric as well.

The pattern is petalled medallions with crowns and pomegranates, deriving from the generic class of *ferronerie* and pomegranate velvets of the fifteenth century. The contrast between the contours of the longer pile and the plain short pile of the group defines the outlines of the motifs. *Ferronerie* and pomegranate patterns also exist in damask and in other colors, but for official use in Venice it was woven only in the pile-on-pile technique in this rich shade of red. The present form as a chasuble was, therefore, its second life, after the officer of state had parted with it.

183

FRENCH

Needlepoint Lace,
Point de France
(detail)

1675–1700
Linen
193 x 39.3 cm. (76 x 15 1/2 in.)
Acquired 1892

Lacemaking in France, under the protection and patronage of Louis XIV, and building on the skills already demonstrated in Italy and Flanders, went on to achieve a perfection which has not been matched anywhere. Because of these ideal conditions, further enhanced by designs from several of the famous painters of the age, great technical and artistic quality was attained and may be seen in the example before us. This piece, from the hands of anonymous artisans, reflects the decorative style of Jean Bérain (1637–1711).

The pattern has four motifs, the first one repeated again at the right with slight variations. The first and last have three miniature portraits in oval frames (the top one upside down to be read from above) and an ornate window that enframes a pair of owls and a night sky where the moon's face is surrounded by stars. Beneath this is a royal crown and below that a trophy of a helmet, banners, and shields, with a *fleur-de-lis* on either side. (This arrangement is reversed on the right.) The next motif (illustrated here) has two men in costume supporting a crown and standing on either side of another figure, who holds up a decorative mace. As they all seem to be wearing feathered headdresses, the supposition is that this is an allegory for the continent of America. The third motif is similar in arrangement, but has winged figures (*genii*) holding a crown over the head of a man in a theatrical costume of half-armor, who holds a mace, possibly an allegory for Europe or an allegorical portrait of Louis XIV. Various minor decorations fill the gaps between these: scrolls, flowering trees set in containers, columns, and vines.

ITALIAN OR FRENCH

Chasuble

1700–25
Silk fancy compound cloth, brocaded
104.1 x 74 cm. (41 x 29 1/4 in.)

Even though this vestment was made for an ecclesiast, it has all the gaiety and style of a fine drapery or bit of royal attire. The effect of these rich colors and patterns is not unlike the impression made by the later eighteenth-century Rococo churches of Bavaria. A floral pattern of leaves and flowers is arranged symmetrically across front and back. Strips of gilt galloon outline a stylized cross and a narrow band of bobbin lace has been added at the neck.

Unlike the other examples of textiles illustrated on these pages, this has a particularly modern feeling, and pieces like it have become prized by collectors in this century for domestic use. Reminiscent as it is of all the sumptousness of the eighteenth century, it also recalls the imaginative floral patterns of the Near East, in material such as that worn by *The Young Lady of Fashion* or in the wall tile shown elsewhere in the book.

186

VENETIAN

Commode

Late seventeenth or early eighteenth
   century
Walnut with ivory and satinwood
   inlay
98 x 141 x 70 cm. (38 5/8 x 55 1/2 x
   27 1/2 in.)
Acquired 1892

This oddly shaped chest with its unusual decoration is a fine example of the crosscurrents of style in Venetian decorative arts. On either side of the central panel on the front, the drawers project out at an angle. The figures are inlaid in ivory and stained satinwood, set against a background of ebonized wood and natural satinwood. The spaces between are inlaid with ivory in scroll designs with tendrils, leaves, and buds. The drawers are framed in black moldings, the same wood used for the feet, and have been fitted with locks and brass pulls.

What appear to be warriors, priests, pilgrims, and allegorical figures inhabit the scenes. On the center of the top drawer, a young man with a feather in his hat is handing objects (bread?) or receiving them from a priest. Below, a priest or ruler is attacked by a warrior, and, at the bottom, two warriors are reaching out to each other. Winged figures with armbands are seated on either end of the drawer fronts, and, on the side panels, a woman in classical dress leans on a cornucopia. The top has a central scene with four persons approaching a sword and shield on the ground, where a man kneels, perhaps in veneration.

Similar inlay and design appear on two cabinets bought with this commode. On these smaller chests the projecting sides end in pilasters supporting herms carved in the round; the center of each drawer has a cartouche of inlaid ivory with bust figures in ink. One set seems to be Oriental, the other classical.

All of these figures and scenes appear to be a mixture of Venetian designers' interpretations of Oriental and classical motifs, the latter used only for the figures of women. The scenes, damaged and therefore difficult to decipher, do not seem related, as none of the figures are repeated.

189

VENETIAN

Painted Chair

Middle of the eighteenth century
Painted wood
109 cm. high (43 in.)

Venetian decorative arts in the eighteenth century borrowed styles from major European countries. The maker of the set of twelve chairs of which this is one example, employed designs from England and France and a version of the *chinoiserie* then popular. The shape of the back is influenced by Queen Anne furniture while the rest of the chair seems modelled on French Regency or Louis XV styles. The chairs are painted, gilded, and decorated in floral, foliate and geometric patterns against a cream or green background, the latter perhaps in imitation of Chinese lacquer. The scenes on the splats, each one different, depict Orientals, men in armor, or ladies in contemporary costume, and these have no particular theme. In this detail we see what appears to be a Chinese man seated below a parasol with a servant waving an incense burner. Only in costume and facial expression could these figures be considered Oriental, as the flowers and designs in the decorative patterns are all based on prevailing European models.

PAUL MANSHIP

b. St. Paul, Minnesota, 1885
d. New York, 1966

Diana

1921
Bronze
68.8 cm. high (27 $^{1}/_{16}$ in.)
Acquired 1921

Among a number of artists whom Mrs. Gardner befriended in later life was the young sculptor Paul Manship. He made a small relief of *Europa and the Bull* for her and sent it with Christmas greetings in 1917. Sketches for the *Diana* were begun the same year, with a pendant sculpture of *Actaeon*, an image in the same pose reversed, in which Actaeon has been shot by the arrow released by Diana.

This bronze was number four of twelve casts made in 1921, and was bought by Mrs. Gardner that year. Manship then produced large casts (eighty-four inches high excluding base and bow) of both pieces which may be found at Brookgreen Gardens, South Carolina, and finally an intermediate size (forty-eight inches high, excluding base and bow). His work often reflected his love for classical sculpture, which he studied in Rome, and in this case, Greek vase painting with its linear definition and silhouette. It was also representative of his own age, characterized by emphasis on movement, smooth surfaces, and stylized anatomy. His success reached a high point in the 1930s, notably with his work in New York for the gates to the Bronx Zoo, the famous gilded figure of *Prometheus* at Rockefeller Center, and his sculpture for the World's Fair of 1939.

CHINESE

Ku, or Beaker

Shang Dynasty, ca. 1200–1100 B.C.
Bronze
26.5 cm. high (10 1/2 in.)
Acquired 1922

Among the oldest objects in the collection and one of the last purchased by Mrs. Gardner, this goblet for wine was recommended to her by her old friend Denman Ross, himself a prodigious collector. The shape was probably derived from vessels made in clay but the casting and surface decoration are examples of the remarkable advances in technique made during the Shang Dynasty.

It is generally believed that vessels of this period were used only by members of the aristocratic ruling class in sacrificial ceremonies, and that the decoration had a religious significance. The pattern in the middle between the concentric circles is divided into quadrants, and two quadrants together may be read as a mask with the raised spots as eyes. In time, the masks became animal faces which, by the second century B.C., were called *t'ao-t'ieh* (literally translated as "monster of greed"). The significance of these is a matter of speculation. The fine spiral decoration, both in the midsection and on the base, is called *yun-lei-wen* (cloud and thunder pattern). Beakers of this period (Shang Style III) follow a similar scheme with eye sockets placed symmetrically in the midsection but in serial order in the base.

The restrained design and olive-green patina enhance the graceful lines of the vessel, allowing the eye to dwell on the serene beauty of its shape. Open slits forming a cross between the lower concentric circles may have been necessary for the process of casting, the technical virtuosity of which, at this point in history, was unequalled outside of China.

194

CHINESE

Two Bears

Han Dynasty, ca. first century B.C.
Bronze
15.5 cm. high (6 1/16 in.)
Acquired 1914

Han Dynasty sculpture took on a realism in the rendering of form and in the lifelike expression implied in the pose. In this case, the bears crouch in an informal position, one leg tucked under the body. The weight of each is on the large forepaws and the neck is extended, the mouth open as though the animal were about to growl. Small ears and eyes barely interrupt the long line of the back which ends at the snout. Although the modelling is simple, the proportions convey the bulk and power of the bears. The patina, which was once gilt on green lacquer, is now mottled but otherwise the bears are intact. One bear has markings on the bottom of two paws, characters which are read as *wang* (king, ruler) and *yu* (right-hand side). The exact significance of this is not known.

It has been suggested that these bears were once tomb treasures, or that they had a symbolic meaning connected with the hunt. Information supplied by the dealer in Paris, who purchased them in Shantung province, places them in Shensi province, where they were discovered in 1900. Two other similar but not identical bears are known, as are a number of bronze animals from the same period.

CHINESE

Votive Stele

Eastern Wei Dynasty 543 A.D.
Limestone
142 x 82 x 63 cm.
  (56 x 32 1/4 x 24 3/4 in.)
Acquired 1914

The inscription on the base of this stele is composed of a dedication and a list of seventy-eight names, and states that the stone image is in honor of the Emperor, the donors' ancestors of seven generations, and their parents now living. The names of fifty-one are listed as inhabitants of the town, including three venerables of the town, and the other twenty-seven are persons who made donations for specific parts of the stele or who contributed to the celebration of its unveiling. The inscribed donations therefore provide information identifying the various figures and scenes.

The Buddha, with his right hand in the gesture of fearlessness, his left in that of charity, wears a sanghati in the Chinese manner, with the inner garment belted high on the waist. The pleats of the robe are indicated by double lines on the shoulder and across the front, among the earliest use of this style in China. All of the five figures in high relief have equally sophisticated treatment. To the Buddha's right and left are attendant monks and the larger divinities, the Bodhisattvas, one with a water bottle, the other with what seems to be a purse. These stand on lotus pedestals supported by a dragon. Above and to the right of the Buddha are the remains of an angelic being suspended in clouds, and directly behind are the rings of the Buddha's halo, the outer one decorated with lotus designs. The Bodhisattvas' halos take the shape of a flame.

The base, carved from a separate stone, has a large lotus in the center. (The lotus is symbolic of transcendency and of the Buddha's power to open the soul to eternal life.) On the top are two lions and an incense burner. The sides and the back are carved with ten spirit kings, three on each side and four on the back. On either side of the inscription are two guardians, one with a flask and the other with a thunderbolt.

The low relief on the back is particularly interesting and refined. In the upper register is a scene from the eleventh chapter of the *Lotus Sutra*, in which Śākyamuni Buddha was suddenly transported into heaven to meet with another Buddha, Prabhūtaratna. Monks kneel below them and two guardian figures stand on lotus pedestals to either side of the central figure. In the lowest register are two lions and an incense burner on a lotus petal. On each of the narrow sides of the stone itself is a standing figure, Kuan-Shih-Yin Bodhisattva, each in a graceful pose.

The inscription also gives the day of the stele's unveiling and the name of the man who provided the feast. The stele probably came from Honan province, where black limestone of this kind was used for sculpture.

199

CHINESE

Kuan-Yin

Eleventh or first half of the twelfth
    century
Polychromed wood with gilt
117 cm. high (46 in.)
Acquired 1919

The Kuan-Yin, or Bodhisattva of Compassion, is shown in "royal ease," as the pose is called in India, the source for all Buddhist sculptural imagery. A sash knotted in front secures the skirt, but the ends of the knot are now missing. The torso is bare except for the necklace and scarf; armlets, bracelets, and crown complete the costume. At one time the figure may have worn a long jewelled chain as well. The hair is piled high on the head with two locks falling on the shoulders. In the crown is an image of Amitabha Buddha seated on a lotus.

The pose depicts Kuan-Yin on a rock on the edge of the water, a pose which appeared in the tenth century in China and was popular into the fourteenth century. The wood was covered with gesso before it was painted and gilded, as with medieval wood sculpture in Europe. Areas of original color remain, and the sculptor has shown a refinement of line in the costume and jewelry. At one time the empty socket in the middle of the forehead held a jewel, crystal or glass, representing the *ūrnā*, or curl of hair from which, according to doctrine, a ray of light emanates.

201

PERSIAN (KASHAN)

Plate with a Scene of Two Lovers

Ca. 1210
Metallic luster pigments on white
   ceramic
35 cm. in diameter (13 7/8 in.)
Acquired 1912

By comparison with other pottery, the source of this plate may be placed in Kashan, a city well known for excellent ceramic products in the thirteenth century. Painted in a reddish-brown luster on a hard white clay, the plate has an undulating edge made up of twenty-nine cusps, and an inner band of repetitive devices, inside which there is a shallow side ending in the flat center with its medallion and a band of white bearing an inscription.

In the medallion, a woman plays a stringed instrument to entertain her lover. Their richly decorated costumes suggest royalty or members of the royal household. A white bird in flight at the bottom completes the medallion. The decorative bands around the central scene contain writing in a *naskhī* script which does not identify the scene or the source of the plate. However, a plate in the Freer Gallery, Washington, from the same mold gives the name of the artist and the Moslem date corresponding to the year 1210 A.D.

203

TURKISH (IZNIK)

Wall Tile

Last quarter of the sixteenth century
Polychromed underglaze on
  siliceous ceramic
21.5 x 25 cm. (8 1/2 x 9 3/4 in.)
Acquired 1885

This tile was part of a wall decoration made in the ceramic workshops of Iznik in Nicaea during the reign of Sultan Murad III.

Many similar pieces remain on Ottoman buildings of this period, where they are prized for their floral designs and bright colors, particularly the use of tomato red with black, blue, turquoise, and green. This particular tile has an unusual abundance of black, and from the designs in the corners it is possible to reconstruct the appearance of the wall. The grape leaf with flowers painted on it is attached at the center to a vine, which curves through the pattern from top to bottom with cartouches and roundels alternating on either side. The roundel has four tulips and four carnations in a circular pattern on a black ground. The cartouche has a central tulip with hyacinths rising on either side against a white ground.

Probably the tile was once nine and one half inches square, and was cut down to avoid a nicked edge before it appeared in the possession of a dealer in Boston, from whom it was purchased by Mrs. Gardner in 1885. A companion to this from the same wall, and almost identical, has been discovered in a private club in Providence.

JAPANESE SCREEN

The Tale of Genji (detail)

Seventeenth century
Pair of six-fold screens, color on
   gilded paper
170 x 379 cm. (67 x 149 1/4 in.)
Acquired 1903

The Tale of Genji was written circa 1000 A.D. by Lady Murasaki and has since been reprinted in numerous editions up to the present time, so many, in fact, that almost no Western book can equal it. A narrative scroll was made of the story as early as the twelfth century, and thereafter scenes from the novel appeared as screen paintings. Artists who had never read the 54 chapters relied on an abbreviated edition of the fourteenth century in which there is a summary of the characters and descriptions of the costumes in each scene.

The museum owns a pair of screens with five episodes on one and six on the other, each with gold clouds separating the scenes. Against the strong lines of the architecture, the carefully rendered costumes and cultivated trees provide contrasting movement and abstract patterns which lend particular charm to the individual incidents as well as to the overall effect. The work is done in a fine and precise hand by an anonymous artist; an erroneous signature and date were added later.

Reading from right to left, and top to bottom, in this detail, the first scene shows a young girl watching her pet sparrow, which has been set free by a page. Prince Genji, attended by Lord Koremitsu and a page, watches from behind a brushwood fence. Below, the prince and a friend prepare to dance in the garden of a large house, where men sit on the porch and women are seen in adjoining rooms and in the garden below. On the left a carriage has to be pushed out of the way so that another may pass and this leads to a squabble between the grooms.

Index of Artists